WOLVES IN FOLKLORE, RELIGION AND MYTHOLOGY

Books LLC®, Wiki Series, Memphis, USA, 2011. ISBN: 9781156670682. www.booksllc.net
Copyright: http://creativecommons.org/licenses/by-sa/3.0/deed.en

Table of Contents

Werewolves

Aconitum... 1
Agriopas... 5
Airitech.. 5
Beast of Bray Road 6
Beast of Gévaudan 6
Buda (folk religion)........................... 8
Clinical lycanthropy 9
Cynocephaly 10
Damarchus 12
Gilles Garnier 12
Lycanthropy 13
Lycaon (Arcadia) 16
Lykaia 17
Man into Wolf................................. 18
Peter Stumpp................................... 19

Pricolici 19
Rougarou... 19
The Boy and the Wolves 20
Valais witch trials........................... 20
Vârcolac 22
Wepwawet....................................... 22
Werewolf... 23
Werewolf witch trials...................... 29
Wulver... 30

Wolves in Norse mythology

Fenrir.. 31
Geri and Freki 36
Hati Hróðvitnisson 37
Mánagarmr...................................... 37
Sköll 38

Warg.. 38

Wolves in folklore, religion and mythology

Amarok (wolf)................................. 39
Asena... 40
Capitoline Wolf............................... 40
Chechen wolf 41
MacQueen of Pall à Chrocain 42
Marchosias 43
The Boy Who Cried Wolf................ 43
Wolf of Gubbio 44
Wolves in folklore, religion and mythology 45
Wolves in heraldry 48

Introduction

Purchase of this book entitles you to a free trial membership in the publisher's book club at www.booksllc.net. (Time limited offer.) Simply enter the barcode number from the back cover onto the membership form. The book club entitles you to select from hundreds of thousands of books at no additional charge. You can also download a digital copy of this and related books to read on the go. Simply enter the title or subject onto the search form to find them.

Each chapter in this book ends with a URL to a hyperlinked online version. Type the URL exactly as it appears. If you change the URL's capitalization it won't work. Use the online version to access related pages, websites, footnotes, tables, color photos, updates. Click the version history tab to see the chapter's contributors. Click the edit link to suggest changes.

A large and diverse editor base collaboratively wrote the book, not a single author. After a long process of discussion and debate, the chapters gradually took on a neutral point of view reached through consensus. Additional editors expanded and contributed to chapters striving to achieve balance and comprehensive coverage. This reduced the regional or cultural bias found in many other books and provided access and breadth on subject matter otherwise little documented.

Aconitum

Aconitum (/ˌækəˈnaɪtəm/ *A-co-ní-tum*), known as **aconite, monkshood, wolfsbane, leopard's bane, women's bane, Devil's helmet** or **blue rocket**, is a genus of over 250 species of flowering plants belonging to the buttercup family (Ranunculaceae).

Overview

These herbaceous perennial plants are chiefly natives of the mountainous parts of the northern hemisphere, growing in moisture retentive but well draining soils on mountain meadows. Their dark green leaves lack stipules. They are palmate or deeply palmately lobed with 5–7 segments. Each segment again is 3-lobed with coarse sharp teeth. The leaves have a spiral or alternate arrangement. The lower leaves have long petioles.

The tall, erect stem is crowned by racemes of large blue, purple, white, yellow or pink zygomorphic flowers with numerous stamens. They are distinguishable by having one of the five petaloid sepals (the posterior one), called the galea, in the form of a cylindrical helmet; hence the English name monkshood. There are 2–10 petals, in the form of nectaries. The two upper petals are large. They are placed under the hood of the calyx and are supported on long stalks. They have a hollow spur at their apex, containing the nectar. The other petals are small and scale like or non forming. The 3–5 carpels are partially fused at the base.

The fruit is a follicle, a follicle being a dry, unilocular, many-seeded fruit formed from one carpel, and dehiscing by the ventral suture in order to release seeds.

Natural hybrids
- *Aconitum × austriacum*
- *Aconitum × cammarum*
- *Aconitum × hebegynum*
- *Aconitum × oenipontanum* (*A. variegatum* ssp. *variegatum* × ssp. *paniculatum*)
- *Aconitum × pilosiusculum*
- *Aconitum × platanifolium* (*A. lycoctonum* ssp. *neapolitanum* × ssp. *vulparia*)
- *Aconitum × zahlbruckneri* (*A. napellus* ssp. *vulgare* × *A. variegatum* ssp. *variegatum*)

Uses
The roots of *Aconitum ferox* supply the Nepalese poison called *bikh*, *bish*, or *nabee*. It contains large quantities of the alkaloid pseudaconitine, which is a deadly poison. *Aconitum palmatum* yields another of the bikh poisons. The root of *Aconitum luridum*, of the Himalaya, is said to be as poisonous as that of *A. ferox* or *A. napellus*.

Several species of Aconitum have been used as arrow poisons. The Minaro in Ladakh use *A. napellus* on their arrows to hunt ibex, while the Ainu in Japan used a species of Aconitum to hunt bear. The Chinese also used Aconitum poisons both for hunting and for warfare.

Many species of *Aconitum* are cultivated in gardens, having either blue or yellow flowers. *Aconitum lycoctonum* (Alpine wolfsbane) is a yellow-flowered species common in the Alps of Switzerland. As garden plants the aconites are very ornamental, hardy perennial plants. They thrive in the garden soils, and will grow in the shade of trees. They are easily propagated by divisions of the root or by seeds; care should be taken not to leave pieces of the root where livestock might be poisoned.

The most common plant in this genus, *Aconitum napellus* (the Common Monkshood) was considered in the past to be of therapeutic and of toxicological importance. Its roots have occasionally been mistaken for horseradish. When touched to one's lip, the juice of the aconite root produces a feeling of numbness and tingling. This plant is used as a food plant by some Lepidoptera species including Dot Moth, The Engrailed, Mouse Moth, Wormwood Pug, and Yellow-tail.

Traditional uses

Aconitum delphinifolium, monkshood from Alaska

Aconite has long been used in the traditional medicine of Asia (India, China). In Ayurveda the herb is used to increase *pitta* (fire, bile) dosha and to enhance penetration in small doses. However more frequently the herb is detoxified according to the samskaras process and studies, cited in the detoxification section below show that it no longer possesses active toxicity. It is used in traditional Chinese medicine as a treatment for Yang deficiency, "coldness", general debilitation. The herb is considered hot and toxic. It is prepared in extremely small doses. More frequently ginger processed aconite, of lower toxicity, "fu zi" is used. Aconite is one ingredient of Tribhuvankirti, an Ayurvedic preparation for treating a "cold in the head" and fever. Aconite was mixed with patrinia and coix, in a famous treatment for appendicitis described in a formula from the Jingui Yaolue (ca. 220 A.D.) Aconite was also described in Greek and Roman medicine by Theophrastus, Dioscorides, and Pliny the Elder, who most likely prescribed the Alpine species Aconitum lycoctonum. The herb was cultivated widely in Europe, probably reaching England before the tenth century, where it was farmed with some difficulty, but came to be widely valued as an anodyne, diuretic, and diaphoretic. In the nineteenth century much aconite was imported from China, Japan, Fiji, and Tonga, with a number of species used to manufacture alkaloids of varying potency but generally similar effect, most often used externally and rarely internally. Effects of different preparations were standardized by testing on guinea pigs.

In Western medicine preparations of aconite were used until just after the middle of the 20th century, but it is no longer employed as it has been replaced by safer and more effective drugs and treatments. The 1911 British Pharmaceutical Codex regarded the medical uses and toxicity of aconite root or leaves to be virtually identical to that of purified aconitine. Aconite first stimulates and later paralyses/numbs the nerves to the sensations of pain, touch, and temperature if applied to the skin or to a mucous membrane; the initial tingling therefore gives place to a long-continued anaesthetic action. Great caution was required, as abraded skin could absorb a dangerous dose of the drug, and merely tasting some of the concentrated preparations available could be fatal. The local anaesthesia of peripheral nerves can be attributed to at least eleven alkaloids with varying potency and stability.

Internal uses were also pursued, to slow the pulse, as a sedative in pericarditis and heart palpitations, and well diluted as a mild diaphoretic, or to reduce feverishness in treatment of colds, pneumonia, quinsy, laryngitis, croup, and asthma due to exposure. Taken internally, aconite acts very notably on the circulation, the respiration, and the nervous system. The pulse is slowed, the number of beats per minute being actually reduced, under considerable doses, to forty, or even thirty, per minute. The blood-pressure synchronously falls, and the heart is arrested in diastole. Immediately before arrest, the heart may beat much faster than normally, though with extreme irregularity, and in animals the auricles may be observed occasionally to miss a beat, as in poisoning by veratrine and colchicum. The action of aconitine on the circulation is due to an initial stimulation of the cardio-inhibitory centre in the medulla oblongata (at the root of the vagus nerves), and later to a directly toxic influence on the nerve-ganglia and muscular fibres of the heart itself. The fall in blood-pressure is not due to any direct influence on the vessels. The respiration becomes slower owing to a paralytic action on the respiratory centre and, in warm-blooded animals, death is due to this action, the respiration being arrested before the action of the heart. Aconite further depresses the activity of all nerve-terminals, the sensory being affected before the motor. In small doses, it therefore tends to relieve pain, if this is present. The activity of the spinal cord is similarly depressed. The pupil is at first contracted, and afterwards dilated. The cerebrum is totally unaffected by aconite, consciousness and the intelligence remaining normal to the last. The antipyretic action which considerable doses of aconite display is not specific but is the result of its influence on the circulation and respiration and of its slight diaphoretic action.

Toxicology

Marked symptoms may appear almost immediately, usually not later than one hour, and "with large doses death is almost instantaneous." Death usually occurs within 2 to 6 hours in fatal poisoning (20 to 40 mL of tincture may prove fatal). The initial signs are gastrointestinal including nausea, vomiting, and diarrhea. There is followed by a sensation of burning, tingling, and numbness in the mouth and face, and of burning in the abdomen. In severe poisonings pronounced motor weakness occurs and cutaneous sensations of tingling and numbness spread to the limbs. Cardiovascular features include hypotension, bradycardia, sinus tachycardia, and ventricular arrhythmias. Other features may include sweating, dizziness, difficulty in breathing, headache, and confusion. The main causes of death are ventricular arrhythmias and asystole, paralysis of the heart or of the respiratory center. The only post-mortem signs are those of asphyxia.

Treatment of poisoning is mainly supportive. All patients require close monitoring of blood pressure and cardiac rhythm. Gastrointestinal decontamination with activated charcoal can be used if given within 1 hour of ingestion. The major physiological antidote is atropine, which is used to treat bradycardia. Other drugs used for ventricular arrhythmia include lidocaine, amiodarone, bretylium, flecainide, procainamide, and mexiletine. Cardiopulmonary bypass is used if symptoms are refractory to treatment with these drugs. Successful use of charcoal hemoperfusion has been claimed in patients with severe aconite poisoning.

Poisoning may also occur following picking the leaves without wearing gloves; the aconitine toxin is absorbed easily through the skin. From practical experience, the sap oozing from eleven picked leaves will cause cardiac symptoms for a couple of hours. In this event, there will be no gastrointestinal effects. Tingling will start at the point of absorption and extend up the arm to the shoulder, after which the heart will start to be affected. The tingling will be followed by unpleasant numbness. Treatment is similar to poisoning caused by oral ingestion.

Aconitine is a potent neurotoxin that blocks tetrodotoxin-sensitive sodium channels. Pretreatment with barakol 10 mg/kg IV reduces the incidence of aconitine-induced ventricular fibrillation and ventricular tachycardia, as well as mortality. Five µg/kg IV of tetrodotoxin has the same effect. The protective effects of barakol are probably due to the prevention of intracellular sodium ion accumulation.

Canadian actor Andre Noble died during a camping trip on July 30, 2004 after the accidental consumption of aconite from monkshood.

In January 2009, the British 'Curry Killer' Lakhvir Singh, killed her lover Lakhvinder Cheema with a curry dish laced with Indian Aconite. On 11 February 2010 she was sentenced to life imprisonment with a minimum term of 23 years for the murder.

Detoxification

Both Chinese medicine and Ayurveda have methods of processing aconite to reduce its toxicity. In Chinese medicine, the traditional pao zhi or preparation of aconite is to steam it with ginger in a fairly elaborate procedure. Due to the variable levels of toxicity in any given sample of the dried herb, there are still issues with using it. Most but not all cases of aconite toxicity in Taiwan were due to the consumption of unprocessed aconite.

According to an article by the Indian scientists Thorat and Dahanukar, "Crude aconite is an extremely lethal substance. However, the science of Ayurveda looks upon aconite as a therapeutic entity. Crude aconite is always processed i.e. it undergoes 'samskaras' before being utilized in the Ayurvedic formulations. This study was undertaken in mice, to ascertain whether 'processed' aconite is less toxic as compared to the crude or unprocessed one. It was seen that crude aconite was significantly toxic to mice (100% mortality at a dose of 2.6 mg/mouse) whereas the fully processed aconite was absolutely non-toxic (no mortality at a dose even 8 times as high as that of crude aconite). Further, all the steps in the processing were essential for complete detoxification"

Popular culture

Northern Blue Monkshood (*Aconitum noveboracense*)

Aconitum features in literature in a number of instances:
- Wolfsbane has been ascribed with supernatural powers in the mythology relating to werewolves and other lycanthropes, either to repel them, relating to aconite's use in poisoning wolves and other animals, or in some way induce their lycanthropic condition, as aconite was often an important ingredient in witches' magic ointments. In folklore, aconite was also said to make a person into a werewolf if it is worn, smelled, or eaten. They are also said to kill werewolves if they wear, smell, or eat aconite. Other accounts claim Wolfsbane is used as a brew to prolong the lycanthropic condition in the event a werewolf became under the full moon's influence.
- In Greek mythology, Medea attempted to poison Theseus with a cup of wine poisoned with wolfsbane. However Aegeus, his father, interceded when he discerned his identity.
- In an episode of *Home Improvement* wolfsbane is given to Tim by Wilson to help him ward off the bad luck he has been experiencing as a presumed result of throwing out a chain letter.
- In the book *Airman* by Eoin Colfer, Marshall Hugo Bonvilain invites Conor's family to his tower and poisons the wine with wolfsbane which they don't drink.
- Shakespeare, in Henry IV Part II Act 4 Scene 4 refers to aconite, alongside rash gunpowder, working as strongly as the "venom of suggestion" to break up close relationships (cf Iago's role in Othello).
- John Keats, in his Ode on Melancholy, writes:

No, no, go not to Lethe, neither twist Wolf's bane, tight-rooted, for its poisonous wine Nor suffer thy pale forehead to be kissed By nightshade, ruby grape of Proserpine…

- *Aconitum* plays a major role in the story "The Cardinal Napellus" by Gustav Meyrink. It is identified with religious beliefs and connected to the idea of fate.
- Wolfsbane is mentioned in one of the verses of the Wiccan Rede:

Widdershins go when the Moon doth wane, An' the Werewolf howls by the dread Wolfsbane.

- A gypsy poem was written for the Lon Chaney, Jr. series of werewolf movies; it has been quoted in other werewolf movies as well:

Even those who are pure of heart, and say their prayers at night, can become a wolf, when the wolfsbane blooms and the autumn moon is bright.

- In the third book of the Brother Cadfael series, *Monk's Hood*, the herbalist Cadfael uses aconite as an ingredient in a liniment, which is later stolen and used to poison a victim. It is occasionally referenced in other situations as well.
- In Children of the Vampire, the second book in *Jeanne Kalogridis* vampire series, wolfsbane is named as an ingredient for a very powerful elixir designed to transform one into the form of a wolf (or perhaps other creatures as well) so as to commence training to become a vampire-killer.
- Wolfsbane in the Harry Potter series is a toxic plant that can be used as an ingredient in the Wolfsbane Potion, a potion werewolves use to maintain their rationality and conscience when transformed into a wolf. During the events of *Harry Potter and the Prisoner of Azkaban*, the werewolf Remus Lupin forgets to take his dose of Wolfsbane Potion that Severus Snape prepared for him and ends up turning into a werewolf during the full moon. In his first potions class, Harry Potter is mocked by Severus Snape for not knowing that monkshood, wolfsbane, and aconite are the same plant, in an attempt to humiliate him.
- An overdose of aconite was the method in which Rudolph Bloom, father of Leopold Bloom in James Joyce's Ulysses, committed suicide. Rudolph Bloom died... in consequence of an overdose of monkshood (aconite) self-administered in the form of a neuralgic liniment...
- Aconite poisoning is used as a means of disposal in the Alistair MacLean novel *Bear Island*.
- In Brian Jacques's *Redwall* book *Outcast of Redwall*, Veil the ferret uses wolfsbane to poison one of the residents of Redwall Abbey.
- Aconite is also used as a poison in Midsomer Murders, in the episode "Garden of Death".
- In the 1931 film *Dracula*, Wolfsbane is used to keep Dracula out of households.
- Monkshood is used as a plot device in the movie *Ginger Snaps*, as a means of treating lycanthropy.
- A controversial herbal remedy for cancer containing aconite was used by the character Kostoglotov in Aleksandr Solzhenitsyn's novel Cancer Ward.
- The character William Walker, otherwise known as the Wolf Lord, is assassinated, rather appropriately, with aconite in *On the Oceans of Eternity*, the third book in the Nantucket series by S. M. Stirling.
- In Alex Kava's *A Necessary Evil*, character Father Michael Keller is poisoned by monkshood in his tea.
- In the 1998 play by Craig Lucas, *The Dying Gaul*, the main character uses

- the root of a monkshood plant to poison his lover's wife.
- In the British TV series *Heartbeat*, in the first episode of series 8 (1998), the poisonings are eventually found to be due to common monkshood root mistaken for horseradish and made into sauce in the pub.
- It is the namesake for the British alternative metal band Aconite Thrill.
- In the video game nethack, wolfsbane is used as a cure for lycanthropy.
- In the manga and anime *Reborn!* one of the villains is named Torikabuto, which is Japanese for wolfsbane. As a reference to the many names of the wolfsbane such as monkshood and Devil's helmet, Torikabuto is constantly wearing a black hood over his head and a demonic mask on his face.
- Wolfsbane is also supposed to be highly deadly towards vampires.
- In the video game The Elder Scrolls IV: Oblivion, Monkshood can be harvested and used to make potions.
- Hinted at in Stephen King's *Cycle of the Werewolf*, in which Reverend Lowe at some point remembers his lycanthropy might have started after he picked up some strange flowers in a graveyard.
- While legend suggests that Cleopatra, the last queen of Egypt was killed by a snake bite, many historians actually believe that she committed suicide by swallowing a lethal drug cocktail made of opium, aconitum (wolfsbane) and hemlock, a highly poisonous plant from the parsley family.
- In the hit CW TV series *The Vampire Diaries*, Aconitum Vulperia (wolfsbane) is highly toxic to werewolves, similar to the poisonous effects that vervain has on vampires.
- Ino Yamanaka, a character in the anime Naruto, uses Wolfsbane as a weapon, due to its poisonous qualities.
- In the video game Assassins Creed Brotherhood, Aconite is a quest item required to gain access to fast poison.
- Monkshood was used to poison a teenager in episode 3 ("Sympathy for the Devil") of the TV series *Rizzoli & Isles*
- In the new MTV show Teen Wolf, Wolfsbane is used to hide the true identity of the human side in a werewolf. Also a rare form of Monkshood called Nordic Blue Monkshood is extremely toxic to werewolves in the sense that exposure to the plant will kill them overtime, and force transformations.

Gallery

Unidentified Aconitum (possibly *Aconitum carmichaelii*)

Trailing White Monkshood (*Aconitum reclinatum)*

Southern Blue Monkshood (*Aconitum uncinatum*)

Source (edited): "http://en.wikipedia.org/wiki/Aconitum"

Agriopas

Agriopas was a writer of ancient Greece mentioned by Pliny the Elder. He was the author of an account of the Olympic victors, called the *Olympionicae*. His exact date is unknown.

Agriopas is also sometimes cited by writers on werewolf mythology. These writers have handed down Agriopas' tale of Demaenetus of Parrhasia who, during the Arcadian sacrifices for the festival of Zeus Lycaeus, tasted the viscera of a human child, and was turned into a wolf for ten years. At the end of those ten years he supposedly became a man again and competed in the ancient Olympic Games.

"Agriopas" was also in some manuscripts of Pliny given as the name of the father of Cinyras, rather than Apollo. Whether this is genuine or an error remains a matter of some debate.

Source (edited): "http://en.wikipedia.org/wiki/Agriopas"

Airitech

In Irish mythology, **Airitech** was a mysterious character whose three daughters were werewolves. They were eventually killed by Cas Corach. The story appears in *Agallamh na Seanórach*, which is part of the Fenian Cycle.

Source (edited): "http://en.wikipedia.org/wiki/Airitech"

Beast of Bray Road

The **Beast of Bray Road** (or the **Bray Road Beast**) is a cryptozoological creature first reported in the 1980s on a rural road outside of Elkhorn, Wisconsin. The same label has been applied well beyond the initial location, to any unknown creature from southern Wisconsin or northern Illinois that is described as having similar characteristics to those reported in the initial set of sightings.

Bray Road itself is a quiet country road near the community of Elkhorn. The rash of claimed sightings in the late 1980s and early 1990s prompted a local newspaper, the *Walworth County Week*, to assign reporter Linda Godfrey to cover the story. Godfrey initially was skeptical, but later became convinced of the sincerity of the witnesses. Her series of articles later became a book titled *The Beast of Bray Road: Trailing Wisconsin's Werewolf*.

Description

Most descriptions and eyewitness accounts are catalogued in Linda Godfrey's book *Hunting the American Werewolf*.

The Beast of Bray Road is described by purported witnesses in several ways: as a bear-like creature, as a hairy biped resembling Bigfoot, and as an unusually large (2-4 feet tall on all fours, 7 feet tall standing up) intelligent wolf-like creature apt to walk on its hind legs and weighing 400-700 pounds.

Although the Beast of Bray Road has not been seen to transform from a human into a wolf in any of the sightings, it has been labeled a werewolf in newspaper articles.

The Beast of Bray Road is also known as the "Bearcoon" to some Elkhorn residents.

Explanations

A number of animal-based theories have been proposed. They include that the creature is an undiscovered variety of wild dog, a waheela (said to be a giant prehistoric wolf similar to Amarok), or a wolfdog or a coydog.

It is also possible that hoaxes and mass hysteria have caused some falsehoods and sightings of normal creatures to all be artificially lumped under the same label. Concurrently with the sightings in Wisconsin, there was a rash of similar encounters in the neighboring state of Michigan. Following the release of "The Legend", a popular song about the Michigan Dogman in 1987, author Steve Cook received dozens of reports, including photograph and film evidence of the creature. There is no known link between the sightings in adjoining states, other than the similarity of the creature described.

Popular culture

The Beast of Bray Road appears in the television program *Mystery Hunters* as well as several books and a motion picture. Articles about it have appeared in *Weekly World News*. The sightings spawned a 2005 exploitation movie directed by Leigh Scott titled *The Beast of Bray Road*. The History Channel's TV series *MonsterQuest* launched an investigation on the beast, in which all witnesses were subjected to lie detector tests. The polygraph administrator could find no indication that any of the witnesses had fabricated their stories. It has appeared in a season 3 episode of *Lost Tapes*, in which it attacks members of a radical militia.

Source (edited): "http://en.wikipedia.org/wiki/Beast_of_Bray_Road"

Beast of Gévaudan

The **Beast of Gévaudan** (French: *La Bête du Gévaudan*; IPA: [la bɜt dy ʒevɔdɑ̃], Occitan: *La Bèstia de Gavaudan*) is a name given to man-eating wolf-like animals alleged to have terrorized the former province of Gévaudan (modern day *département* of Lozère and part of Haute-Loire), in the Margeride Mountains in south-central France from 1764 to 1767 over an area stretching 90 by 80 kilometres (56 by 50 mi). The beasts were consistently described by eyewitnesses as having formidable teeth and immense tails. Their fur had a reddish tinge, and was said to have emitted an unbearable odour. They killed their victims by tearing at their throats with their teeth. The number of victims differs according to source. De Beaufort (1987) estimated 210 attacks, resulting in 113 deaths and 49 injuries; 98 of the victims killed were partly eaten. An enormous amount of manpower and resources was used in the hunting of the animals, including the army, conscripted civilians, several nobles, and a number of royal huntsmen. All animals operated outside of ordinary wolf packs, though eyewitness accounts indicate that they sometimes were accompanied by a smaller female, which did not take part in the attacks. The story is a popular subject for cryptozoologists.

History

Woman defending herself from the Beast of Gévaudan, 18th century print.

Attacks

The first attack that provided a description of one of the creatures took place on 1 June 1764. A woman from Langogne saw a large, lupine animal emerge from the trees and charge directly toward her, but it was driven away by the farm's bulls.

On 30 June, the first official victim of the beast was Jeanne Boulet, 14, killed near the village of Les Hubacs, not far from Langogne.

The beast also seemed to target people over farm animals; many times it would attack someone while cattle were in the same field.

On 12 January 1765, Jacques Portefaix and six friends, including two girls, were attacked by the Beast; they drove it away by staying grouped together. Their fight caught the attention of King Louis XV, who awarded 300 livres to Portefaix, and another 300 livres to be shared among the others. He also directed that Portefaix be educated at the state's expense. The King had taken a personal interest in the attacks, and sent professional wolf-hunters, Jean Charles Marc Antoine Vaumesle d'Enneval and his son Jean-François, to kill the beast. They arrived in Clermont-Ferrand on 17 February 1765, bringing with them eight bloodhounds which had been trained in wolf-hunting. They spent several months hunting wolves, believing them to be the beast. However the attacks continued, and by June 1765 they were replaced by François Antoine (also wrongly named Antoine de Beauterne), the king's harquebus bearer and Lieutenant of the Hunt. He arrived in Le Malzieu on 22 June.

Antoine killing the Wolf of Chazes, 18th-century engraving.

On 21 September 1765, Antoine killed a large grey wolf measuring 80 centimetres (31 in) high, 1.7 metres (5.6 ft) long, and weighing 60 kilograms (130 lb). The wolf was called *Le Loup de Chazes*, after the nearby Abbaye des Chazes. It was agreed locally that this was quite large for a wolf. Antoine officially stated: "We declare by the present report signed from our hand, we never saw a big wolf that could be compared to this one. Which is why we estimate this could be the fearsome beast that caused so much damage." The animal was further identified as the culprit by attack survivors, who recognized the scars on the creature's body, inflicted by victims defending themselves. The wolf was stuffed and sent to Versailles where Antoine was received as a hero, receiving a large sum of money as well as titles and awards.

However, on 2 December 1765, another beast emerged in *la Besseyre Saint Mary*, severely injuring two children. Dozens more deaths are reported to have followed.

Death of the second beast

The killing of the creature that eventually marked the end of the attacks is credited to a local hunter, Jean Chastel, at the Sogne d'Auvers on 19 June 1767. Later novelists (Chevalley, 1936) introduced the idea that Chastel shot it with a blessed silver bullet of his own manufacture. Upon being opened, the animal's stomach was shown to contain human remains.

Controversy surrounds Chastel's account of his success. Family tradition claimed that, when part of a large hunting party, he sat down to read the Bible and pray. During one of the prayers the creature came into sight, staring at Chastel, who finished his prayer before shooting the beast. This would have been aberrant behavior for the beast, as it would usually attack on sight. Some believe this is proof Chastel participated with the beast, or even that he had trained it. However, the story of the prayer may simply have been invented out of religious or romantic motives.

Identity of the beasts

The wolf shot by François Antoine on 21 September 1765, displayed at the court of Louis XV

Various explanations were offered at the time of the attacks as to the beast's identity. Suggestions ranged from exaggerated accounts of wolf attacks, to a werewolf, all the way to the beast being a punishment from God. Jay M. Smith, in his book "Monsters of the Gévaudan," suggests that the deaths attributed to the beast were more likely the work of a number of wolves or packs of wolves.

Suggested species

Richard H. Thompson, author of *Wolf-Hunting in France in the Reign of Louis XV: The Beast of the Gévaudan*, contended that there can be satisfactory explanations based on large wolves for all the Beast's depredations.

Another explanation is that the beasts were some type of domestic dog or crosses between wild wolves and domestic dogs, on account of their large size and unusual coloration. This speculation has found support from naturalist Michel Louis, author of the book *La bête du Gévaudan: L'innocence des loups* (English: The Beast of Gévaudan: The innocence of wolves) and an episode of *Animal X*. Louis wrote that Jean Chastel was frequently seen with a large red coloured mastiff, which he believes sired the beast. He explains that the beast's resistance to bullets may have been due to it wearing the armoured hide of a young boar, thus also accounting for the unusual colour. He dismisses hyenas as culprits, as the beast itself had 42 teeth, while hyenas have 34.

Certain cryptozoologists suggest that

the Beast might be a surviving remnants of a Mesonychid seeing how some witnesses described it as a huge wolf having hooves rather than paws and it was larger than any normal sized wolf.:

In October 2009, the History Channel aired a documentary called *The Real Wolfman* which argued that the beast was an exotic animal in the form of an Asian Hyena, a long haired species of Hyaenidae now extinct in Europe.

In the arts and popular culture

Robert Louis Stevenson traveled through the region in 1878 and described the incident in his book *Travels with a Donkey in the Cévennes*, in which he claims that at least one of the creatures was a wolf:

For this was the land of the ever-memorable Beast, the Napoleon Bonaparte of wolves. What a career was his! He lived ten months at free quarters in Gévaudan and Vivarais; he ate women and children and 'shepherdesses celebrated for their beauty'; he pursued armed horsemen; he has been seen at broad noonday chasing a post-chaise and outrider along the king's high-road, and chaise and outrider fleeing before him at the gallop. He was placarded like a political offender, and ten thousand francs were offered for his head. And yet, when he was shot and sent to Versailles, behold! a common wolf, and even small for that. In the Patricia Briggs novel *Hunting Ground*, the Beast is a French werewolf named Jean Chastel, who has a penchant for hunting women and weak people.

There are two recent films based on the attacks of the Beast: *Brotherhood of the Wolf* (2001), directed by Christophe Gans, and *La bête du Gévaudan* (2003), directed by Patrick Volson.

Brotherhood of the Wolf took several creative liberties in order to make the story more entertaining. Rather than a wolf or wolf-dog crossbreed, the movie portrays the creature as a strange beast equipped with armor to make it seem more threatening. The Beast is the instrument of the film's titular secret organization, which attempts to undermine public confidence in the king and ultimately take over the country by stating that the Beast is a divine punishment for the King's indulgence of the modern embrace of science over religion.

In episode six of the 2011 MTV drama "Teen Wolf", the character Allison learns that her werewolf hunting family was responsible for slaughtering The Beast of Gévaudan while doing a research project for school.

Source (edited): "http://en.wikipedia.org/wiki/Beast_of_G%C3%A9vaudan"

Buda (folk religion)

Buda (or **bouda**), in Ethiopian folk religion, is the power of the evil eye and the ability to change into a hyena. Buda is generally believed to be a power held and wielded by those in a different social group, for example among the Beta Israel or metalworkers. The belief is also present in Sudan, Tanzania, and among the Berber people in Morocco.

Belief in the evil eye, or buda, is widespread in Ethiopia. The Beta Israel, or Ethiopian Jews, are often characterized as possessing buda. Other castes such as ironworkers are often labeled as bearing the buda. In fact, the word for manual worker, *tabib*, is also used to denote "one with the evil eye." The alleged evil power of the tabib is believed to be at a level similar to that of witches.

Buda's alleged prevalence among outsiders correlates with the traditional belief that evil eye curses themselves are rooted in envy. As such, those allegedly possessing the power of buda might do so because of malevolent spirits. One study specifies that they are believed to be "empowered by evil spirit". Niall Finneran describes how "the idea of magical creation underpins the perception of artisans in Ethiopia and in the wider African context. In many cases these skills have been acquired originally from an elemental source of evil via the paternal lineage, rather like a Faustian pact." The power of the evil eye allows its bearer to change into a hyena, allowing him or her to attack another person while concealing his or her human identity.

Some Ethiopian Christians carry an amulet or talisman, known as a *kitab*, or will invoke God's name, to ward off the ill effects of buda. A *debtera*, who is either an unordained priest or educated layperson, will create these protective amulets or talismans.

Ethiopian Orthodox priests continue to intervene and perform exorcisms on behalf of those believed to be afflicted by demons or buda. Such persons are brought to a church or prayer meeting. Amsalu Geleta, in a modern case study, relates elements that are common to Ethiopian Christian exorcisms:

It includes singing praise and victory songs, reading from the Scripture, prayer and confronting the spirit in the name of Jesus. Dialogue with the spirit is another important part of the exorcism ceremony. It helps the counselor (exorcist) to know how the spirit was operating in the life of the demoniac. The signs and events mentioned by the spirit are affirmed by the victim after deliverance.

The exorcism is not always successful, and Geleta notes another instance in which the usual methods were unsuccessful, and the demons apparently left the subject at a later time. In any event, "in all cases the spirit is commanded in no other name than the name of Jesus."

Source (edited): "http://en.wikipedia.org/wiki/Buda_(folk_religion)"

Clinical lycanthropy

Clinical lycanthropy is defined as a rare psychiatric syndrome that involves a delusion that the affected person can transform or has transformed into an animal or that he or she is an animal. Its name is connected to the mythical condition of lycanthropy, a supernatural affliction in which people are said to physically shapeshift into wolves. The terms *zoanthropy* and *therianthropy* are also sometimes used for the delusion that one has turned into an animal in general and not specifically a wolf.

Symptoms

Affected individuals report a delusional belief that they are in the process of transforming into an animal or have already transformed into an animal. It has been linked with the altered states of mind that accompany psychosis (the reality-bending mental state that typically involves delusions and hallucinations) with the transformation only seeming to happen in the mind and behavior of the affected person.

A study on lycanthropy from the McLean Hospital reported on a series of cases and proposed some diagnostic criteria by which lycanthropy could be recognised:
- A patient reports in a moment of lucidity or looking back that he sometimes feels as an animal or has felt like one.
- A patient behaves in a manner that resembles animal behavior, for example crying, grumbling, or creeping.
- A patient may voice their belief in being an animal.

According to these criteria, either a delusional belief in current or past transformation or behavior that suggests a person thinks of themselves as transformed is considered evidence of clinical lycanthropy. The authors go on to note that, although the condition seems to be an expression of psychosis, there is no specific diagnosis of mental or neurological illness associated with its behavioural consequences.

It also seems that lycanthropy is not specific to an experience of human-to-wolf transformation; a wide variety of creatures have been reported as part of the shapeshifting experience. A review of the medical literature from early 2004 lists over thirty published cases of lycanthropy, only the minority of which have wolf or dog themes. Canines are certainly not uncommon, although the experience of being transformed into a hyena, cat, horse, bird or tiger has been reported on more than one occasion. Transformation into frogs, and even bees, has been reported in some instances. A 1989 case study described how one individual reported a serial transformation, experiencing a change from human, to dog, to horse, and then finally cat, before returning to the reality of human existence after treatment. There are also reports of people who experienced transformation into an animal only listed as "unspecified".

Proposed mechanisms

Clinical lycanthropy is a rare condition and is largely considered to be an idiosyncratic expression of a psychotic episode caused by another condition such as schizophrenia, bipolar disorder or clinical depression.

However, there are suggestions that certain neurological and cultural influences may lead to the expression of the human-animal transformation theme that defines the condition.

Neurological factors

One important factor may be differences or changes in parts of the brain known to be involved in representing body shape (e.g., see proprioception and body image). A neuroimaging study of two people diagnosed with clinical lycanthropy showed that these areas display unusual activation, suggesting that when people report their bodies are changing shape, they may be genuinely perceiving those feelings. Body image distortions are not unknown in mental and neurological illness, so this may help explain at least part of the process. One further puzzle is why an affected person does not simply report that their body "feels like it is changing in odd ways", rather than presenting with a delusional belief that they are changing into a specific animal. There is much evidence that psychosis is more than just odd perceptual experiences, so perhaps lycanthropy is the result of these unusual bodily experiences being understood by an already confused mind, perhaps sifted through cultural traditions and ideas.

Source (edited): "http://en.wikipedia.org/wiki/Clinical_lycanthropy"

Cynocephaly

A cynocephalus. From the *Nuremberg Chronicle* (1493).

"Doghead" redirects here. For other meanings, see Doghead (disambiguation).

The condition of **cynocephaly**, having the head of a dog — or of a jackal— is a widely attested legendary phenomenon existing in many different forms and contexts.

Etymology

Cynocephaly is taken from the Latin word *cynocephalus*, meaning "doghead", which derives from Greek: κῠνοκέφᾰλοι. The prefix "cyno-" comes from the combining form of Greek: κύων meaning "dog". This prefix forms compound words having "the sense of dog". The suffix "-cephalic" comes from the Latin word *cephalicus*, meaning "head". This word finds its roots in Greek: κεφαλικός (kephalikos) meaning "capital" from Greek: κεφαλή (kephalē) meaning "head". The suffix "-cephaly", specifically, means "a specific condition or disease of the head". This together forms "a dog-like condition or disease of the head". The phrase cynocephaly also gave birth to the term *cynomorph* which means "dog-like". This phrase is used primarily as *Cynomorpha*, a sub-group of the family Cercopithecidae. This family of primates are known as "dog-like apes" and contain many species of macaques and baboons.

Ancient Greece and Egypt

Cynocephaly was familiar to the Ancient Greeks from representations of the Egyptian gods Hapi (the son of Horus) and Anubis (the Egyptian god of the dead). The Greek word *(Greek: κῠνοκέφᾰλοι)* "dog-head" also identified a sacred Egyptian baboon with the face of a dog.

Reports of dog-headed races can also be traced back to Greek antiquity. In the fifth century BC, the Greek physician Ctesias wrote a detailed report on the existence of cynocephali in India. Similarly, the Greek traveller Megasthenes claimed to know about dog-headed people in India who lived in the mountains, communicated through barking, wore the skins of wild animals and lived by hunting.

Late Antiquity

The "cynocephali" offered such an evocative image of the magic and brutality deemed characteristic of bizarre people of distant places, that it kept returning in medieval literature. Augustine of Hippo mentioned the Cynocephali in City of God, Book XVI, Chapter 8, in the context of discussing whether such beings were descendants of Adam; he considered the possibility that they might not exist at all, or might not be human (which Augustine defines as being a mortal and rational animal: *homo, id est animal rationale mortale*), but insisted that if they were human they were indeed descendants of Adam.

Medieval East

Cynocephali also figure in medieval Christian world-views. A legend that placed St. Andrew and St. Bartholomew among the Parthians presented the case of "Abominable", the citizen of the "city of cannibals... whose face was like unto that of a dog." After receiving baptism, however, he was released from his doggish aspect.

Cynocephalus St. Christopher

Saint Christopher

In the Eastern Orthodox Church, certain icons covertly identify Saint Christopher with the head of a dog. The background to the dog-headed Christopher is laid in the reign of the Emperor Diocletian, when a man named *Reprebus*, *Rebrebus* or *Reprobus* (the "reprobate" or "scoundrel") was captured in combat against tribes dwelling to the west of Egypt in Cyrenaica. To the unit of soldiers, according to the hagiographic narrative, was assigned the name *numerus Marmaritarum* or "Unit of the Marmaritae", which suggests an otherwise-unidentified "Marmaritae" (perhaps the same as the Marmaricae Berber tribe of Cyrenaica). He was reported to be of enormous size, with the head of a dog instead of a man, apparently a characteristic of the Marmaritae. This Byzantine depiction of St. Christopher as dog-headed resulted from their misinterpretation of the Latin term Cananeus to read canineus, that is, "canine."

The German bishop and poet Walter of Speyer portrayed St. Christopher as a giant of a cynocephalic species in the land of the Chananeans (the "canines" of Canaan in the New Testament) who ate human flesh and barked. Eventually, Christopher met the Christ child, regretted his former behavior, and received baptism. He, too, was rewarded with a human appearance, whereupon he devoted his life to Christian service and became an athlete of God, one of the soldier-saints.

Cynocephali illustrated in the Kievan psalter, 1397

Medieval West

Paul the Deacon mentions cynocephali in his *Historia gentis Langobardorum*: "They pretend that they have in their camps Cynocephali, that is, men with dogs' heads. They spread the rumor among the enemy that these men wage war obstinately, drink human blood and quaff their own gore if they cannot reach the foe." At the court of Charlemagne the Norse were given this attribution, implying un-Christian and less-than-human qualities: "I am greatly saddened" said the King of the Franks, in Notker's *Life*, "that I have not been thought worthy to let my Christian hand sport with these dog-heads." The ninth-century Frankish theologian Ratramnus wrote a letter, the *Epistola de Cynocephalis*, on whether the Cynocephali should be considered human. Quoting St. Jerome, Thomas of Cantimpré corroborated the existence of Cynocephali in his *Liber de Monstruosis Hominibus Orientis*, xiv, ("Book of Monstrous men of the Orient"). The thirteenth-century encyclopedist Vincent of Beauvais acquainted his patron Saint Louis IX of France with "an animal with the head of the dog but with all other members of human appearance… Though he behaves like a man… and, when peaceful, he is tender like a man, when furious, he becomes cruel and retaliates on humankind".

In Anglo-Saxon England, the Old English word *wulfes heafod* ("wolf's head") was a technical term for an outlaw, who could be killed as if he were a wolf. The so-called *Leges Edwardi Confessoris*, written around 1140, however, offered a somewhat literal interpretation: "[6.2a] For from the day of his outlawry he bears a wolf's head, which is called *wluesheued* by the English. [6.2b] And this sentence is the same for all outlaws." Cynocephali appear in the Old Welsh poem *Pa Gur?* as *cinbin* (dogheads). Here they are enemies of King Arthur's retinue; Arthur's men fight them in the mountains of *Eidyn* (Edinburgh), and hundreds of them fall at the hand of Arthur's warrior Bedwyr (later known as Bedivere). The next lines of the poem also mention a fight with a character named Garwlwyd (Rough-Gray); a Gwrgi Garwlwyd (Man-Dog Rough-Gray) appears in one of the Welsh Triads, where he is described in such a way that scholars have discussed him as a werewolf.

High and late medieval travel literature

Medieval travellers Giovanni da Pian del Carpine and Marco Polo both mention cynocephali. Giovanni writes of the armies of Ogedei Khan who encounter a race of dogheads who live north of the Dalai-Nor (Northern Ocean), or Lake Baikal. Polo's *Travels* mentions the dog-headed barbarians on the island of Angamanain, or the Andaman Islands. For Polo, although these people grow spices, they are nonetheless cruel and "are all just like big mastiff dogs".

According to Henri Cordier, the source of all the fables of the dog-headed barbarians, whether European, Arabic, or Chinese, can be found in the Alexander Romance.

China

Additionally, in the Chinese record *History of the Liang Dynasty* (Liang Shu), the Buddhist missionary Hui-Sheng describes an island of dog-headed men to the east of Fusang, a nation he visited variously identified as Japan or the Americas. The *History of Northern Dynasties* of Li Yanshou, a Tang dynasty historian, also mentions the 'dog kingdom'.

Modern appearances

Template:Popculture The use of dog-headed, human-bodied characters is still very strong in modern literature. In the domain of comics publishing in North America and in Europe many works feature an "all-cynocephalic" cast or use the heads of dogs and other animals together for social comment or other purposes.

- In the Pulitzer Prize winning graphic novel *Maus* by Art Spiegelman, Jews have human bodies and the heads of mice while characters with their roots in the United States have human bodies and the heads of dogs, Germans have the heads of cats, and the French have the heads of frogs.
- The comic book *Ghost Rider* features a villain named Doghead. He is an anthropomorphic dog who serves Blackheart, the son of Mephisto, the Marvel Comics version of the devil.
- The hero of *Baudolino*, a novel by Umberto Eco, has to face dog-headed people at the end of his journey.
- At the beginning of *A Dog's Head*, a novel by Jean Dutourd, a woman gives birth to a child with a dog's head.
- Dog-headed creatures based on the ancient accounts appear in many modern role-playing games, beginning with the Gnolls of *Dungeons & Dragons*, though it should be noted that Gnoll's heads are based on hyenas, which are not canines.
- The Talmud states that at the time before the Messiah, the "face of the generation will have the face of a dog."

- The Chinese legend of Fu Xi included variations where he had a dog's head, or he and his sister Nu Wa had ugly faces.
- In the USA there are tales of dog-headed creatures, including the Michigan Dogman, and the wolf-like Beast of Bray Road of Wisconsin.
- The Wulver of the Scottish Shetland Isles.
- Psoglav in Serbian mythology.
- The Nacumerians, in *The Voyage and Travels of Sir John Mandeville*.

Related phenomena
- Theriocephaly, the generic term for human-shaped bodies with animal heads
- Werewolves, which figure in archaic Greek and other European traditions.
- Ulfheðnar

Source (edited): "http://en.wikipedia.org/wiki/Cynocephaly"

Damarchus

The Boxer of Quirinal (Museo delle Terme, Rome)

Damarchus or **Damarch** (Greek: Δάμαρχος; fl. ~400 BC) was a victorious Olympic boxer from Parrhasia (Arcadia) said to have changed his shape into that of a wolf at the sacrifice of Lycaean Zeus, becoming a man after nine years.

Source (edited): "http://en.wikipedia.org/wiki/Damarchus"

Gilles Garnier

Gilles Garnier (died January 18, 1573) was a French hermit and cannibalistic, serial murderer convicted of being a werewolf. Alternately known as "The Hermit of St. Bonnot" and "The Werewolf of Dole".

The Werewolf of Dole, Gilles Garnier was a reclusive hermit living outside the town of Dole in the Franche-Comté Province in France. He had recently been married and moved his new wife out to his isolated home. Being unaccustomed to feeding more than just himself he found it difficult to provide for his wife causing discontent between them. During this period several children went missing or were found dead and the authorities of the Franche-Comté province issued an edict encouraging and allowing the people to apprehend and kill the werewolf responsible. One evening a group of workers traveling from a neighboring town came upon what they thought in the dim light to be a wolf but what some recognized as the hermit with the body of a dead child. Soon after Giles Garnier was arrested.

Confession
According to his testimony at trial, while Garnier was in the forest hunting one night trying to find food for himself and his wife, a spectre appeared to him offering to ease his troubles and gave him a magic ointment that would allow him to change into the form of a wolf, making it easier to hunt. Garnier confessed to have stalked and murdered at least four children between the ages of 9 and 12. In October 1572, his first victim was a 10-year-old girl whom he dragged into a vineyard outside of Dole. He

strangled her, removed her clothes, and ate the flesh from her thighs and arms. When he had finished he removed some flesh and took it home to his wife. Weeks later Garnier savagely attacked another girl, biting and clawing her, but was interrupted by passersby and fled.

The girl succumbed to her injuries a few days later. In November, Garnier killed a 10-year-old boy, again cannibalizing him by eating from his thighs and belly and tearing off a leg to save for later. Finally, he strangled another boy but was interrupted for the second time by a group of passersby. He had to abandon his prey before he could eat from it.

Garnier was found guilty of "crimes of lycanthropy and witchcraft" and burned at the stake.

Source (edited): "http://en.wikipedia.org/wiki/Gilles_Garnier"

Lycanthropy

Lycanthropy is the ability or power of a human being to undergo transformation into a werewolf, or to gain wolf-like characteristics. The term comes from Greek *lykanthropos* (Λυκανθρωποσ): λυκος, *lykos* ("wolf") + ανθρωπος, *anthrōpos* ("human"). The word lycanthropy is sometimes used generically for any transformation of a human into animal form, though the precise term for that is technically "therianthropy". Sometimes, "zoanthropy" is used instead of "therianthropy". The word has also been linked to Lycaon, a king of Arcadia who, according to Ovid's *Metamorphoses*, was turned into a ravenous wolf in retribution for attempting to serve human flesh (his own son) to visiting Zeus in an attempt to disprove the god's divinity.

A more modern use of the word is in reference to a mental illness called lycanthropy in which a patient believes he or she is, or has transformed into, an animal and behaves accordingly. This is sometimes referred to as clinical lycanthropy to distinguish it from its use in legends.

Causes

The most common cause of lycanthropy in myths is to be bitten or physically marked by another lycanthrope, although this condition can also be hereditary. Other mythical lycanthropy is not given any specific cause other than being generally attributed to magic, which may be voluntary (a supernatural power) or involuntary (a curse).

Some causes are person-chosen. Anybody has the ability to change into another form with practice. Most people only have one form and this being has been with them somehow some way. Many websites have information how people can and do change into a new form.

Clinical Lycanthropy (where one believes that he or she is a lycanthrope) is a mental disorder, and thus has real psychological causes, as contrasted to legendary lycanthropy.

Mechanisms of transformation

Even if the denotation of lycanthropy is limited to the wolf-metamorphosis of living human beings, the beliefs classed together under this head are far from uniform, and the term is somewhat capriciously applied. The transformation may be temporary or permanent; the were-animal may be the man himself metamorphosed; may be his double whose activity leaves the real man to all appearance unchanged; may be his soul, which goes forth seeking whom it may devour, leaving its body in a state of trance; or it may be no more than the messenger of the human being, a real animal or a familiar spirit, whose intimate connection with its owner is shown by the fact that any injury to it is believed, by a phenomenon known as repercussion, to cause a corresponding injury to the human being.

Transmigration of souls

Lycanthropy is often confused with transmigration; but the essential feature of the were-animal is that it is the alternative form or the double of a living human being, while the soul-animal is the vehicle, temporary or permanent, of the spirit of a dead human being. Nevertheless, instances in legend of humans reincarnated as wolves are often classed with lycanthropy, as well as these instances being labeled werewolves in local folklore.

There is no line of demarcation, and this makes it probable that lycanthropy is connected with nagualism and the belief in familiar spirits, rather than with metempsychosis, as E. B. Tylor argued, or with totemism, as suggested by J. F. M'Lennan. Thus, these origins for lycanthropy mingle a belief in reincarnation, a belief in the sharing of souls between living humans and beasts and a belief in human ghosts appearing as non-human animals after death. A characteristic of metempsychosis is a blurring of the boundaries between the intangible and the corporeal, so that souls are often conceived of as solid, visible forms that need to eat and can do physical harm.

Witchcraft

The phenomenon of repercussion, the power of animal metamorphosis or of sending out a familiar, real or spiritual, as a messenger. The supernormal powers conferred by association with such a familiar are also attributed to the paranormal. Some superstitions found in Witchcraft can be close to lycanthropic beliefs, the occasional involuntary character of lycanthropy being almost the sole distinguishing feature. In another direction the phenomenon of repercussion is asserted to manifest itself in connection with the bush-soul of the West African and the *nagual* of Central America; but though there is no line of demarcation to be drawn on logical grounds, the assumed power of the magician and the intimate association of the bush-soul or the *nagual* with a human being are not termed lycanthropy. Nevertheless it will be well to touch on both these beliefs here.

Symptoms

Lycanthropy can begin when one believes that he/she is destined to take a form of something. Usually this happens in a time of vulnerability, such as after a wedding, death, or major change. Often, the transformation is triggered by someone saying something, doing something, something that makes the victim believe that he/she must begin transformation, such as someone they truly love being in danger. Sometimes, the victim even reads something that makes them believe that they should change form. Usually, the process begins with dry skin, fatigue, and the need to be alone. Slowly, cravings will change and the victim's body will begin to undergo the metamorphosis. Eyes may change shape, hands will change, and hair and eye will gradually change color.

Animal ancestors

Stories of humans descending from animals are common explanations for tribal and clan origins. Sometimes the animals assumed human forms in order to ensure their descendants retained their human shapes, other times the origin story is of a human marrying a normal animal.

North American indigenous traditions particularly mingle the idea of bear ancestors and ursine shapeshifters, with bears often being able to shed their skins to assume human form, marrying human women in this guise. The offspring may be monsters with combined anatomy, they might be very beautiful children with uncanny strength, or they could be shapeshifters themselves.

P'an Hu is represented in various Chinese legends as a supernatural dog, a dog-headed man, or a canine shapeshifter that married an emperor's daughter and founded at least one race. When he is depicted as a shapeshifter, all of him can become human except for his head. The race(s) descended from P'an Hu were often characterized by Chinese writers as monsters who combined human and dog anatomy.

In Altaic mythology of the Turkic and Mongolian peoples, the wolf is a revered animal. The shamanic Turkic peoples even believed they were descendants of wolves in Turkic legends. The legend of Asena is an old Turkic myth that tells of how the Turkic people were created. In Northern China a small Turkic village was raided by Chinese soldiers, but one small baby was left behind. An old she-wolf with a sky-blue mane named Asena found the baby and nursed him, then the she-wolf gave birth to half wolf, half human cubs therefore the Turkic people were born.

Animal spirits

In North and Central America, and to some extent in West Africa, Australia and other parts of the world, every male acquires at puberty a tutelary spirit (see Demonology); in some Native American tribes the youth kills the animal of which he dreams in his initiation fast; its claw, skin or feathers are put into a little bag and become his "medicine" and must be carefully retained, for a "medicine" once lost can never be replaced. In West Africa this relation is said to be entered into by means of the blood bond, and it is so close that the death of the animal causes the man to die and vice versa. Elsewhere the possession of a tutelary spirit in animal form is the privilege of the magician. In Alaska the candidate for magical powers has to leave the abodes of men; the chief of the gods sends an otter to meet him, which he kills by saying "O" four times; he then cuts out its tongue and thereby secures the powers which he seeks.

The Malays believe that the office of *pawang* (priest) what in the worldis only hereditary if the soul of the dead priest, in the form of a tiger, passes into the body of his son. While the familiar is often regarded as the alternative form of the magician, the *nagual* or bush-soul is commonly regarded as wholly distinct from the human being. Transitional beliefs, however, are found, especially in Africa, in which the power of transformation is attributed to the whole of the population of certain areas. The people of Banana are said to change themselves by magical means, composed of human embryos and other ingredients, but in their leopard form they may do no harm to mankind under pain of retaining forever the beast shape. In other cases the change is supposed to be made for the purposes of evil magic and human victims are not prohibited.

A further link is supplied by the Zulu belief that the magician's familiar is really a transformed human being; when he finds a dead body on which he can work his spells without fear of discovery, the wizard breathes a sort of life into it, which enables it to move and speak, it being thought that some dead wizard has taken possession of it. He then burns a hole in the head and through the aperture extracts the tongue. Further spells have the effect of changing the revivified body into the form of some animal, hyena, owl or wild cat, the latter being most in favour. This creature then becomes the wizard's servant and obeys him in all things; its chief use is, however, to inflict sickness and death upon persons who are disliked by its master.

In Melanesia there is a belief in the *tamaniu* or *atai* which is an animal counterpart to a person. It can be an eel, a shark, a lizard, or some other creature. This creature is corporeal, can understand human speech, and shares the same soul as its master, leading to legends which have many characteristics typical of shapeshifter tales, such as any death or injury affecting both forms at once.

Regional varieties

Although the term lycanthropy properly speaking refers to metamorphosis into a wolf (see werewolf), lycanthropy is in popular practice used of transformation into any animal, even though the proper term is therianthropy. In India and the Asian islands the tiger is the most common form; in North Europe, the bear (see berserker); in Japan, the fox, tanuki (raccoon dog), and sometimes a wolf; in Africa, the leopard, hyena, or lion; and in South America, the jaguar. Though there is a tendency for the most important carnivorous animal of the area to take the first place in stories and beliefs as to transformation, the less important beasts of prey and even harmless animals like the deer or rabbit also figure prominently among the were-animals. Other cases are the were-shark of Polynesia and were-crocodile of Indonesia and Egypt.

North America

Many Native cultures feature skinwalkers or a similar concept, wherein a shaman or warrior may, according to cultural tradition, take on an animal form. Animal forms vary accordingly with cultures and local species (including bears and wolves), for example, a coyote is more likely to be found as a skinwalker's alternate form in the Great Plains region. Skinwalkers tend to be totemic.

In modern folklore and fiction the Wendigo found in the stories of many Algonquian peoples is sometimes considered to be similar to lycanthropes, in that humans could transform into a non-human form. The original legends varied significantly, however, with Wendigo sometimes being described as giants made of ice, or hairy beasts, or having other forms.

The Cajuns of Louisiana also believed in a similar creature with the variant name of Rougarou.

There are some modern reports of man-wolf creatures, including the Beast of Bray Road.

South America

According to K. F. P. v. Martius the *kanaima* is a human being who employs poison to carry out his function of blood avenger; other authorities represent the *kanaima* as a jaguar, which is either an avenger of blood or the familiar of a cannibalistic sorcerer. The Europeans of Brazil hold that the seventh child of the same sex in unbroken succession becomes a were-man or woman, and takes the form of a horse (or a mule), a goat, a guará-wolf and a pig. The Brazilian werewolf is mostly related to the Portuguese belief, which includes the werewolf being forced to perform a series of religious duties.

The dolphin-man (boto encantado) is common in native North-Brazilian folklore. However, the myth more likely stems from one of the supposed powers of the boto (wherein it changes its shape into that of a human) rather than a man changing his form into that of an animal.

Europe

The wolf is the most common form of the were-animal, though in the north the bear disputes its pre-eminence. In ancient Greece the dog was also associated with the belief. The were-boar variant is known through Greece and Turkey. Marcellus of Sida, who wrote under the Antonines, gives an account of a disease which befell people in February; but a pathological state seems to be meant.

Romanian folklore actually has multiple variations on the lycanthropy theme. The *vârcolac* is often - though not exclusively - seen as a werewolf though it can refer also to (usually wolf-like) demons, vampires, goblins or ghosts as well; the *pricolici* is more universally wolf-like, and much like the *strigoi* is said to be a formerly human member of the undead, having risen from the grave to wreak havoc on the living. Additionally, both the terms *strigoi* and *moroi* are traditionally closely associated with both *pricolici* and *vârcolaci*, and while modern fiction makes a clear distinction between the terms (with *strigoi* and *moroi* being in usage more a reference to the vampiric than the lycanthropic, and the latter in turn referring more to "living" as opposed to undead vampires), older folklore leaves them not always so easily differentiated, especially with regional variants.

Africa

In Abyssinia the power of transformation is attributed to the Boudas, and at the same time we have records of pathological lycanthropy (see below). Blacksmiths are credited with magical powers in many parts of the world, and it is significant that the Boudas are workers in iron and clay; in the *Life of N. Pearce* (i. 287) a European observer tells a story of a supposed transformation which took place in his presence and almost before his eyes; but it does not appear how far hallucination rather than coincidence must be invoked to explain the experience. The animal forms taken in Africa include the gazelle, crocodile, hippopotamus, hyena, jackal, elephant, lion and leopard.

See: Crocotta

South Pacific

There are various tales of people becoming sharks in various South Pacific islands. For the most part, these were creatures are benevolent or at least not malign. There are several variant stories on how sharks came about. One story is that a were shark inherits their ability. Others point to children lost at sea or children adopted by a shark god. Many of the humans-turned-sharks are described as having skin patterns that no natural sharks have: similar to the cloth patterns of blankets that are wrapped around infants.

East Indies

The Poso-Alfures of central Sulawesi believe that man has three souls, the *inosa*, the *angga* and the *tanoana*. The *inosa* is the vital principle; it can be detected in the veins and arteries; it is given to man by one of the great natural phenomena, more specifically the wind. The *angga* is the intellectual part of man; its seat is unknown; after death it goes to the under-world, and, unlike the *inosa,* which is believed to be dissolved into its original elements, takes possession of an immaterial body. The *tanoana* is the divine in man and after death returns to its lord, Poewempala boeroe. It goes forth during sleep, and all that it sees it whispers into the sleeper's ear and then he dreams. According to another account, the *tanoana* is the substance by which man lives, thinks and acts; the *tanoana* of man, plants and animals is of the same nature. A man's *tanoana* can be strengthened by those of others; when the *tanoana* is long away or destroyed the man dies. The *tanoana* seems to be the soul of which lycanthropic feats are asserted.

Among the Toradjas of central Sulawesi it is believed that a man's "inside" can take the form of a cat, wild pig, ape, deer or other animal, and afterwards resume human form; it is termed *lamboyo*. The exact relation of the *lamboyo* to the *tanoana* does not seem to be settled; it will be seen below that the view seems to vary. According to some the power of transformation is a gift of the gods, but others hold that lycanthropy is contagious and may be acquired by eating food left by a lycanthrope or even by leaning one's head against the same pillar. The Todjoers hold that any one who touches blood becomes a shapeshifter. In accordance with this view is the belief that lycanthropy can be cured; the breast and stomach of the shapeshifter must be rubbed and pinched, just as when any other witch object has to be extracted. The patient drinks medicine, and the contagion leaves the body in the form of snakes and worms. There are certain marks by which a shapeshifter can be recognized. His eyes are unsteady and sometimes green with dark shadows underneath. He does not sleep soundly and fireflies come out of his mouth. His lips remain red in spite of betel chewing, and he has a long tongue. The Todjoers add that his hair stands on end.

Some of the forms of the *lamboyo* are distinguishable from ordinary animals by the fact that they run about among the houses; the were-buffalo has only one horn, and the were-pig transforms itself into an ants' nest, such as hangs from trees. Some say that the lycanthrope does not really take the form of an animal himself, but, like the sorcerer, only sends out a messenger. The *lamboyo* attacks by preference solitary individuals, for he does not like to be observed. The victim feels sleepy and loses consciousness; the *lamboyo* then assumes human form (his body being, however, still at home) and cuts up his victim, scattering the fragments all about. He then takes the liver and eats it, puts the body together again, licks it with his long tongue and joins it together. When the victim comes to himself again he has no idea that anything unusual has happened to him. He goes home, but soon begins to feel unwell. In a few days he dies, but before his death he is able sometimes to name the shapeshifter to whom he has fallen a victim.

From this account it might be inferred that the *lamboyo* was identical with the *tanoana*: the absence of the *lamboyo* seems to entail a condition of unconsciousness, and it can assume human form. In other cases, however, the *lamboyo* seems to be analogous to the familiar of the sorcerer. The Toradjas tell a story of how a man once came to a house and asked the woman to give him a rendezvous; it was night and she was asleep; the question was put three times before the answer was given "in the tobacco plantation". The husband was awake, and next day followed his wife, who was irresistibly drawn thither. The lycanthrope came to meet her in human form, although his body was engaged in building a new house, and caused the woman to faint by stamping three times on the ground. Thereupon the husband attacked the shapeshifter with a piece of wood, and the latter to escape transformed himself into a leaf; this the husband put into a piece of bamboo and fastened the ends so that he could not escape, he then went back to the village and put the bamboo in the fire. The shapeshifter said "Don't", and as soon as it was burnt he fell dead.

In another case a woman died, and, as her death was believed to be due to the malevolence of a lycanthrope, her husband watched by her body. For, like Indian witches, the werewolf, for some reason, wishes to revive his victim and comes in human form to carry off the coffin. As soon as the woman was brought to life the husband attacked the werewolf, who transformed himself into a piece of wood and was burnt. The woman remained alive, but her murderer died the same night.

According to a third form of the belief, the body of the shapeshifter is itself transformed. One evening a man left the hut in which a party were preparing to pass the night; one of his companions heard a deer and fired into the darkness. Soon after the man came back and said he had been shot. Although no marks were to be seen he died a few days later. Source (edited): "http://en.wikipedia.org/wiki/Lycanthropy"

Lycaon (Arcadia)

For the Trojan Lycaon, see Lycaon (son of Priamos).

Zeus turning Lycaon into a wolf; engraving by Hendrik Goltzius.

Lycaon was a king of Arcadia, son of Pelasgus and Meliboea, who in the most popular version of the myth tested Zeus and as a punishment was transformed into the form of a wolf.

Versions of the Myth

There are several version of the Lycaon-myth, already reported by Hesiod (*Fragmenta astronomica*, by Eratosthenes, *Catasterismi*), told by several authors. The most popular version is the one reported by Ovid in the first book of his *Metamorphoses*.

The different versions of the myth are as follows:

- According to Pausanias VIII Lycaon was instantly transformed into a wolf after sacrificing a child on the altar of Zeus and sprinkling the blood on the altar.
- According to Apollodor Lycaon had sired 50 sons with many wives. These sons were the most nefarious and carefree of all people. To test them Zeus visited them in the shape of a poor peon. They mixed the entrails of a child under the god's meal, whereupon the enraged Zeus threw over the table with the meal, which explains the name of the city

Trapezus, and killed Lycaon and his sons with lightning. Only the youngest son was saved due to the intervention of the earth-goddess Ge.
- According to Lykophron all were transformed into wolves.
- According to Hyginus Jupiter came to Lycaon because of his daughter Callisto. In this version only Lycaon was transformed into a wolf and his sons were killed by lightning.
- Nicolas Damascenus tells that Lycaon's sons were nefarious. To test Zeus they mixed the flesh of a boy under the sacrifices, whereupon all who were present during the murder of the child were killed by lightning.
- According to Ovid it was only Lycaon who served Zeus the flesh of a prisoner, partly cooked and partly roasted. Thereupon Zeus brought the roof down and transformed the fleeing Lycaon into a wolf.
- According to Eratosthenes Lycaon butchered his grandson, who was put together again by Zeus and placed upon the constellations.

Sons of Lycaon

According to the Bibliotheca (Pseudo-Apollodorus), the 50 sons of Lycaon were:

Maenalus was in early modern times being represented by the now obsolete constellations Mons Maenalus in the southern part of Boötes.

An alternate list of Lycaon's sons is given by Pausanias. According to his account, almost each of them founded a city in Arcadia and became its eponym.

1. Nyctimus succeeded to Lycaon's power
2. Pallas founded Pallantium
3. Orestheus, Oresthasium
4. Phigalus, Phigalia
5. Trapezeus, Trapezous
6. Daseatas, Dasea
7. Macareus, Macaria
8. Helisson, town of Helisson (also gave his name to a nearby river)
9. Acacus, Acacesium
10. Thocnus, Thocnia
11. Orchomenus, Orchomenus and Methydrium
12. Hypsus, Hypsus
13. (name missing), Melaneae
14. Thyreus, Thyraeum
15. Maenalus, Maenalus
16. Tegeates, Tegea
17. Mantineus, Mantinea
18. Cromus, Cromi
19. Charisius, Charisia
20. Tricolonus, Tricoloni
21. Peraethus, Peraetheis
22. Aseatas, Asea
23. (name missing, Lyceus?), Lycoa
24. Alipherus, a city of his name
25. Heraeus, a city of his name
26. Oenotrus (the youngest), Oenotria in Italy

Plutarch gives the names of two sons that stayed aside from the abomination: Eleuther and Lebadus.

Source (edited): "http://en.wikipedia.org/wiki/Lycaon_(Arcadia)"

Lykaia

In Ancient Greece, the **Lykaia** (Greek: Λυκαία) was an archaic festival with a secret ritual on the slopes of Mount Lykaion ("Wolf Mountain"), the tallest peak in rustic Arcadia. The rituals and myths of this primitive rite of passage centered upon an ancient threat of cannibalism and the possibility of a werewolf transformation for the *epheboi* (adolescent males) who were the participants. The festival occurred yearly, probably at the beginning of May.

The epithet *Lykaios* ("wolf-Zeus") is assumed by Zeus only in connection with the Lykaia, which was the main Arcadian festival. Zeus had only a formal connection as patron of the ritual. In the founding myth, of Lycaon's banquet for the gods that included the flesh of a human sacrifice, perhaps one of his sons, Nyctimus or his grandson, Arcas, Zeus overturned the table and struck the house of Lyceus with a thunderbolt; his patronage at the Lykaia can have been little more than a formula. Long afterward, in the late 3rd century CE, the philosopher Porphyry reported that Theophrastus had compared the sacrifice "at the Lykaia in Arcadia" with Carthaginian sacrifices to Moloch.

The ritual was nocturnal, to judge from the name of Nyctimus (*nyx*, "night") that was given to the son of Lycaeus who was killed and served up as part of the feast to Zeus. Rumors of the ceremony that circulated among other Greeks revolved around the theme of human sacrifice and cannibalism: according to Plato, a particular clan would gather on the mountain to make a sacrifice every nine years to Zeus Lykaios, and a single morsel of human entrails would be intermingled with the animal's. Whoever ate the human flesh was said to turn into a wolf, and could only regain human form if he did not eat again of human flesh until the next nine-year cycle had ended. The traveller Pausanias told of an Olympic boxing champion Damarchus of Parrhasia, who had "turned into a wolf at the sacrifice to Zeus Lykaios, and changed back into a man again in the ninth year thereafter", from which Walter Burkert affirms that, for Damarchus to have successfully participated at least nine years later, the participants in the ritual feast must have been ephebes.

There were several sites. At the summit on Mount Lykaion Pausanias saw the ash-pile altar to Zeus but, as attending the rite was impossible, he was obliged to "let it be as it is and as it was from the beginning".

Near the ancient ash-heap where the sacrifices took place was a forbidden precinct in which, allegedly, no shadows were ever cast. Anyone who entered would have to be sacrificed. There was the cave of Rhea, the *Kretaia*, where, according to local legend, Zeus was born and was cared for by the nymphs. There were games associated with the satisfactory completion of the Lykaia, which removed in the 4th century to Megalopolis; when it was founded in 371 BCE, Megalopolis was the first urbanization in rustic Arcadia;

there the major temple was dedicated to Zeus Lykaios, though the Arcadians continued to sacrifice on the mountain-top to Pausanias' day (2nd century CE).

Modern archaeologists have found no trace of human remains among the sacrificial detritus, but recent discoveries at the mountain-top ash-heap altar that Pausanias saw but was reluctant to pry into, reveal that it was much older than the Classical Greeks themselves realised. Early 20th century excavations at the site had revealed nothing earlier than ca. 700 BCE, but the Greek-American interdisciplinary Mt. Lykaion Excavation and Survey Project excavated a trench and detected ritual presence at the site at the beginning of the third millennium BCE, a thousand years before Zeus was worshiped in Greece. A Late Minoan rock crystal seal bearing the image of a bull was a notable surprise.

Apollo Lykaios

Apollo, too had an archaic wolf-form, *Apollo Lycaeus*, worshipped in Athens at the Lykeion, or Lyceum, which was made memorable as the site where Aristotle walked and taught.

Lykaian Pan

A sanctuary of Pan was also located upon the mountain. According to tradition, Euandros, son of Hermes, led a colony from Pallantion in Arkadia into Italy, where he built a town Pallantion on the Palatine, and introduced the cult of Pan Lýkaios and the festival of the Lykaia, which later became the major Roman festival of Lupercalia.

Modern Lykaia

The lighting of the flame at Lykaia in August 2005

In 1973, the Ano Karyes Association "Lykaios Dias" established the modern Lykaia, which are held every four years on the same place as the ancient games. The motto of these games is "Stefanites and not Chrimatites" (Greek: "Στεφανίτες" και όχι "Χρηματίτες"), meaning that the purpose of these games is solely the moral perfection of man and not rewarding the winners with pecuniary means. Modern Lykaia are usually held in the beginning of August. The games begin with the lighting of the flame on the Arcadian's sacred peak. The Estiades of Mount Lykaion, making their appearance from the north, bring the Arcadian's eternal flame. The first Estiada walks slowly towards the southern pillar base (where two golden eagles were placed in ancient times) and lights the torch. The head priestess recites the Lycean Ode by Pindarus and then gives the torch to an athlete named as torch-bearer. The torch-bearer then runs into the stadium and lights the altar which is placed there. The closing ceremony includes cultural events, the lowering of the flag and the playing of the Greece's national anthem. The winner of each athletic event is awarded with an olive branch, a cup, a tripod, a medal or a diploma. All the athletes who participated-regardless of their performance-receive a certificate of participation, thus justifying the Games' motto. The last Lykaia were held from the 29th of July to the 7th of August 2005. The next games took place in the summer of 2009.

Source (edited): "http://en.wikipedia.org/wiki/Lykaia"

Man into Wolf

Man Into Wolf; An Anthropological Interpretation of Sadism, Masochism and Lycanthropy is a book by Robert Eisler, published in 1948 . The text is based upon his readings in archeology and anthropology; anything not covered by these disciplines is then dealt with using Jungian methods of dream analysis and the theory of archetypes. For instance, his remarks concerning the nature of life in prehistory are largely derived from his interpretations of the dreams of psychotherapy patients.

Subject matter

Eisler begins with an investigation into sadism and masochism which concludes that people seek not pleasure so much as strong sensations. Whether one seeks strong pleasurable sensations, unpleasurable ones, or some combination thereof depends on which group of apes one is descended from.

He asserts that humanity evolved from two groups of apes: one peaceful, vegetarian and practicing free love; the other violent, carnivorous and given to fighting over sex partners. Originally all were of the former group. However, Eisler argues that Ice Age food shortages caused some to imitate wolves and other beasts of prey, wearing animal skins and taking up hunting. He claims this is the historical basis of the werewolf legends found in many cultures.

Eisler advocates a return to what he imagines was the harmonious life of the earliest primates and proposes the development of a new psychology and ultimately a new society, lest we are destroyed in a nuclear war brought about by descendants of the wolf-men.

Source (edited): "http://en.wikipedia.org/wiki/Man_into_Wolf"

Peter Stumpp

Peter Stumpp (died 1589) (whose name is also spelt as **Peter Stube**, **Pe(e)ter Stubbe**, **Peter Stübbe** or **Peter Stumpf**) was a German farmer, accused of being a serial killer and a cannibal, also known as the "Werewolf of Bedburg".
Source (edited): "http://en.wikipedia.org/wiki/Peter_Stumpp"

Pricolici

A **Pricolici** (same form in plural) is a werewolf also Vampire in Romanian folklore. Similar to a vârcolac, although the latter sometimes symbolises a goblin, whereas the pricolici always has wolf-like characteristics.

Pricolici, like strigoi, are undead souls that have risen from the grave to harm living people. While a strigoi possesses anthropomorphic qualities similar to the ones it had before death, a pricolici always resembles a wolf or large dog. Malicious, violent men are often said to become pricolici after death, in order to continue harming other humans.

Some Romanian folklore delineates that Pricolici are werewolves in life and after they die, return as vampires. This also gives rise to the legend of vampires can turn into animals such as wolves, cats, or owls and (rarely) bats. The common theme of all these animals being that they are nocturnal hunters much like vampires.

Even as recently as modern times, many people living in rural areas of Romania have claimed to have been viciously attacked by abnormally large and fierce wolves. Apparently, these wolves attack silently, unexpectedly and only solitary targets. Victims of such attacks often claim that their aggressor wasn't an ordinary wolf, but a pricolici who has come back to life to continue wreaking havoc.

The etymology of the word is unknown.
Source (edited): "http://en.wikipedia.org/wiki/Pricolici"

Rougarou

The **Rougarou** (alternately spelled as **Roux-Ga-Roux**, **Rugaroo**, or **Rugaru**), is a legendary creature in Laurentian French communities linked to European notions of the werewolf.

Versions

The stories of the creature known as a rougarou are as diverse as the spelling of its name, though they are all connected to francophone cultures through a common derived belief in the **Loup-garou** (French pronunciation: [lu ɡaˈʁu], English: /ˈluː ɡəˈruː/). *Loup* is French for wolf, and *garou* (from Frankish *garulf,* cognate with English werewolf) is a man who transforms into an animal.

Louisiana folklore

A traditional Cajun Courir de Mardi Gras costume based on a Rougaroo (figure on left)

Rougarou represents a variant pronunciation and spelling of the original French *loup-garou*. According to Barry Jean Ancelet, an academic expert on Cajun folklore and professor at the University of Louisiana at Lafayette, the tale of the rougarou is a common legend across French Louisiana. Both words are used interchangeably in southern Louisiana. Some people call the monster *rougarou*; others refer to it as the *loup garou*.

The rougarou legend has been spread for many generations, either directly from French settlers to Louisiana (New France) or via the French Canadian immigrants centuries ago.

In the Cajun legends, the creature is said to prowl the swamps around Acadiana and Greater New Orleans, and possibly the fields or forests of the regions. The rougarou most often is described as a creature with a human body and the head of a wolf or dog, similar to the werewolf legend.

Often the story-telling has been used to inspire fear and obedience. One such example is stories that have been told by elders to persuade Cajun children to behave. According to another variation, the wolf-like beast will hunt down and kill Catholics who do not follow the rules of Lent. This coincides with the French Catholic loup-garou stories, according to which the method for turning into a werewolf is to break Lent seven years in a row.

A common blood sucking legend says that the rougarou is under the spell for 101 days. After that time, the curse is transferred from person to person when the rougarou draws another human's blood. During that day the creature returns to human form. Although acting sickly, the human refrains from telling others of the situation for fear of being killed.

Other stories range from the rougarou as a headless horseman to the rougarou being derived from witchcraft. In the latter claim, only a witch can make a rougarou—either by turning into a wolf herself, or by cursing others with lycanthropy.

Native American folklore

The creature, spelled **Rugaru**, has been associated with Native American legends, though there is some dispute. Such folklore versions of the rugaru vary from being mild bigfoot (sasquatch) creatures to cannibal-like Native American wendigos. Some dispute the connection between Native American folktales and the francophone rugaru.

As is the norm with legends transmitted by oral tradition, stories often contradict one another. The stories of the wendigo vary by tribe and region, but the most common cause of the change is typically related to cannibalism.

A modified example, not in the original wendigo legends, is that if a person sees a rugaru, that person will be transformed into one. Thereafter, the unfortunate victim will be doomed to wander in the form of this monster. That rugaru story bears some resemblance to a Native American version of the wendigo legend related in a short story by Algernon Blackwood. In Blackwood's fictional adaptation of the legend, seeing a wendigo causes one to turn into a wendigo.

It is important to note that *rugaru* is not a native Ojibwa word, nor is it derived from the languages of neighboring Native American peoples. However, it has a striking similarity to the French word for werewolf, *loup garou*.

It's possible the Turtle Mountain Ojibwa or Chippewa in North Dakota picked up the French name for "hairy human-like being" from the influence of French Canadian trappers and missionaries with whom they had extensive dealings. Somehow that term also had been referenced to their neighbors' stories of bigfoot.

Author Peter Matthiessen argues that the rugaru is a separate legend from that of the cannibal-like giant wendigo. While the wendigo is feared, he notes that the rugaru is seen as sacred and in tune with Mother Earth, somewhat like bigfoot legends are today.

Though identified with bigfoot, there is little evidence in the indigenous folklore that it is meant to refer the same or a similar creature.

In popular culture

The English version of the creature was recently used in TV series Supernatural. In the series, it was featured for one episode (4.04, "Metamorphosis") and was a creature that was human-like but possessed superhuman abilities and a taste for human flesh that could not be satisfied. It was also mentioned in the fifth season finale (5.22, "Swan Song") in the conclusion, and in the opening scene of a sixth season episode (6.10, "Caged Heat").

A version of this creature was noted in The Dresden Files book Fool Moon describing the *Loup-garou* as one of three types of werewolves, very similar to the type described above.

The Audubon Zoo in New Orleans has an exhibit on the Rougarou and features a life-sized mannequin of what the Rougarou might look like.

Rougarou is also the title of an online literary journal published out of the University of Louisiana at Lafayette.
Source (edited): "http://en.wikipedia.org/wiki/Rougarou"

The Boy and the Wolves

The Boy and the Wolves is a Native American fairy tale. Andrew Lang included it in *The Yellow Fairy Book*.

Synopsis

A man lived far from his people, but one day he died. He told his older children that they must never forsake their younger brother. Soon after, their mother died, extracting the same promise.

The older brother left one day, abandoning his sister and younger brother. Later, his sister left, leaving much food and promising to come back for him, but she found her older brother with their people, married, and she also married and forgot their younger brother.

When the boy had eaten all that his sister left, he went out and ate from what the wolves killed.

One day, the older brother heard a voice singing, "My brother, my brother! I am becoming a wolf, I am becoming a wolf!" He tried to find him, but he heard wolves howl and saw his brother turn into a wolf and run off with them. He went home and mourned the rest of his life.
Source (edited): "http://en.wikipedia.org/wiki/The_Boy_and_the_Wolves"

Valais witch trials

The **Valais witch trials** consisted of a witch-hunt including a series of witch trials which took place in the Duchy of Savoy in today's southeastern France and Switzerland between 1428 and 1447. It can be considered as the first series of witch trials in Europe, fifty years before the starting point of European witch trials. The victims were also accused of being werewolves. The persecutions started in French-speaking Valais and spread to German-speaking

Valais (Wallis) and nearby valleys in both the French and German-speaking Alps. The number of the victims of the persecutions is unknown; there were at least 367 people killed of both genders.

Background

In 1428, the duchy of Savoy had been tormented by a civil war from 1415-1419, between clans of the nobility, where people had been severed between the sides for and against the Raron family, which other noble clans had rebelled against, and society was in a state of great tension.

On 7 August 1428, delegates from seven districts in Valais demanded that the authorities initiate an investigation against alleged, unknown witches and sorcerers. Anyone denounced as a sorcerer by more than three people was to be arrested. If they confessed, they were to be burned at the stake as heretics, and if they did not confess, they would be tortured until they did so. Also, those pointed out by more than two of the judged sorcerers were to be arrested.

The events began in Val d'Anniviers and Val d'Hérens in southern French-speaking Valais and spread north to the German-speaking Valais (Wallis). Within one and a half years, between one and two hundred people had been burned to death. The hysteria had by then spread to the French and Swiss Alps, from Sankt Bernhard, Thuringia in Savoy to Briançon in Dauphiné. From these territories, it then spread over the valleys in Drance, Argentière, Freissinières and Valpute, resulting in one hundred and ten women and fifty seven men being tortured or burned to death, until the persecutions stopped in 1447.

The witch trials of Valais are poorly documented; the best source is the contemporary chronicle made by the clerk of the court, Johannes Fründ, (1400-1469), an eyewitness to the events. His document, however, was written in the middle of the trials (circa 1430, seventeen years before their termination), and therefore lacks a complete coverage.

Quotations from the trials

The following are citations from the chronicles of Johannes Fründ:
" In the year which was counted one thousand and four hundred and thereafter the twenty eight year after the birth of Christ, the bishopric of Wallis saw the uprising of evil, murder and heresy among witches and sorcerers, among women as well as men, known by the name sortilegi in Latin, and they were found first in two valleys in Wallis..."

" ...and an abundance of them have confessed to great evil and many murders and heretic beliefs and an abundance of evil things, which they have performed, such things which are in Latin known as sortilegia, and of which many are stated in this document; however, a lot of it is not mentioned, so that no one may be corrupted. One should consider that these people, be they male or female, which are guilty of these things and this evil which they have performed, have learned this from the evil spirit..."

"There were even those who killed their own children and fired and cooked them and took them to their company to eat them, and carried mischief and other things to church, so that everyone believed them to be children. But they had left their children at home and ate them later, when they so chose."

" There have also been many of them, guilty of such evil, so great a heresy and so many murders, that they with this evil, heresy and magic did not tell any to the priest, so that it may not be stopped. And there were many of these people, who could speak more when they had been apprehended than other uneducated people, and who called upon God and his saints more than others. This they did so that they would be considered innocent. And some of them did not confess at all; some let themselves be tormented and tortured to death, rather than confess or say anything...."

"...and still they were many testimonies against them and even more had reported them as guilty, which everyone could give proof of, and they were thought bewitched so not to be able to point out the other witches. And no matter how severely they were questioned, during more and more torture, many would no confess but let themselves be tortured. So they died from it, and were all the same judged and burned, some alive and some dead. "

" And there had been so many, that they claimed that if they had been able to rule but one year more, they could have established a court among themselves; and the evil spirit lead them to understand that they would be so strong that they need not fear no rule or court and that they would establish a court to take control over Christianity ..."

"...for they revealed they condemned over seven hundred people, of which over two hundred have been burned in one and a half years; they are still sentenced and burned every day, when you are able to arrest them."

The procedure

People with a good reputation pointed out by a condemned were not arrested directly but first investigated discreetly. However, those pointed out by several condemned were arrested immediately. Some confessed directly; others refused and were described as very verbal in their defense. Only very few of their names are known, but they were all peasants, though some of them were described as well educated and learned.

With the exception of the trials in Dauphiné, where most accused were female, there were about as many male as female among the accused. They are not considered to have been old, as they managed to withstand torture long before they died. People were arrested daily.

Accusations

- Flying: to have smeared in chairs, flying through the air and plundering wine cellars.
- Lycanthropy: to have killed cattle in the shapes of werewolves.
- Invisibility: to have made themselves invisible with herbs.
- To have cured sickness and paralysis caused by sorcery by giving it to someone else.
- Cannibalism: to have abducted and eaten children.
- Curses.

- To have met and learned magic from Satan.
- Conspiracy: to have planned depriving Christianity of its power over humanity.

The Devil was to have come to sinners and promised to teach them magic if they renounced Christianity and stopped going to church and confession; they paid him taxes and he did not demand any worshipping.

The executions

The condemned was tied upon a ladder with a wooden crucifix in their arms and a bag of gunpowder around their neck. The ladder was then tipped into the burning stake. Some were instead decapitated before being burned. Many were tortured to death but their bodies were burned at the stake nonetheless.

The property of the executed was given to their family only if they could swear to have been unaware of the sorcery; otherwise it went to the nobility, who paid for the executions of their vassals. When Fründ wrote his document in 1430, 100 or 200 people had been executed but the persecutions were to continue until 1447. It's hard to know the exact number of victims by that time. Unlike later trials, about as many men as women are believed to have been killed.

Source (edited): "http://en.wikipedia.org/wiki/Valais_witch_trials"

Vârcolac

A **vârcolac** in Romanian folklore may refer to several different figures. In some versions, a vârcolac is a wolf demon, which, like the Norse Hati and Sköll, occasionally swallows the moon and the sun, and is thus responsible for eclipses. It may also refer to a wizard that has the power to turn into a wolf for camouflage. This so-called **vârcolac** had magical powers that made him be feared by local men who thus called him a demon.

Other legends say it is a ghost or vampire (*Strigoi*) while a third group of traditions say it is a werewolf (in some versions, a werewolf that emerges from the corpses of babies). In Romanian, vârcolac commonly means "werewolf". It can occasionally mean "goblin".

The word *vârcolac* is a loan from Slavic (cf. Bulgarian *vărkolak*, Serbian *vukodlak*), originally meaning "werewolf" (etymologically "Wolf's Fur"). However, the term has come to denote mostly vampires in Balkan Slavic folklore. Nevertheless, the idea that the *vârkolak* is a wolf that swallows the sun and the moon is also attested in North-Western Bulgaria. See also *Vrykolakas* for more details about the word. Another possible source is the Latin "vermicolacius", as mentioned by Ovid, which literally translates as "twisted worm".

The *pricolici* is another form of vârcolac, also resembling a werewolf.

Source (edited): "http://en.wikipedia.org/wiki/V%C3%A2rcolac"

Wepwawet

In late Egyptian mythology, **Wepwawet** (hieroglyphic *wp-w3w.t*; also rendered **Upuaut**, **Wep-wawet**, **Wepawet**, and **Ophois**) was originally a war deity, whose cult centre was Asyut in Upper Egypt (Lycopolis in the Greco-Roman period). His name means, *opener of the ways*. Some interpret that Wepwawet was seen as a scout, going out to clear routes for the army to proceed forward. One inscription from the Sinai states that Wepwawet "opens the way" to king Sekhemkhet's victory.

Wepwawet originally was seen as a wolf deity, thus the Greek name of Lycopolis, meaning *city of wolves*, and it is likely the case that Wepwawet was originally just a symbol of the pharaoh, seeking to associate with wolf-like attributes, that later became deified as a mascot to accompany the pharaoh. Likewise, Wepwawet was said to accompany the pharaoh on hunts, in which capacity he was titled *(one with) sharp arrow more powerful than the gods*.

Over time, the connection to war, and thus to death, led to Wepwawet also being seen as one who opened the ways to, and through, duat, for the spirits of the dead. Through this, and the similarity of the jackal to the wolf, Wepwawet became associated with Anubis, a deity that was worshiped in Asyut, eventually being considered his son. Seen as a jackal, he also was said to be Set's son. Consequently, Wepwawet often is confused with Anubis. This deity appears in the Temple of Seti I at Abydos.

In later Egyptian art, Wepwawet was depicted as a wolf or a jackal, or as a man with the head of a wolf or a jackal. Even when considered a jackal, Wepwawet usually was shown with grey, or white fur, reflecting his lupine origins. He was depicted dressed as a soldier, as well as carrying other military equipment—a mace and a bow.

For what generally is considered to be lauding purposes of the pharaohs, a later myth briefly was circulated claiming that Wepwawet was born at the sanctuary of Wadjet, the sacred site for the oldest goddess of Lower Egypt that is located in the heart of Lower Egypt. Consequently, Wepwawet, who had hitherto been the standard of Upper Egypt alone, formed an integral part of royal rituals, symbolizing the unification of Egypt.

In the late pyramid texts, Wepwawet is called "Ra" who has gone up from the horizon, perhaps as the "opener" of the sky. In the later Egyptian funerary context, Wepwawet assists at the Opening of the mouth ceremony and guides the deceased into the netherworld.

It would appear that a lack of comprehension of the animal species native to Egypt led European Egyptologists to mistake the deity Wewawet for a Jackal even while the Ancient Egyptians clearly identified it as a Wolf.

The Egyptian Jackal (Canis aureus lupaster) also known as the African Wolf or Wolf Jackal is currently listed as a subspecies of the golden jackal but molecular and osteological data has established that is a unique species in its own right. It is native to Egypt, Libya, and Ethiopia, though its post Pleistocene range once encompassed the Palestine region.

Its closest relatives are the Abyssinian Wolf, also known as the Red Wolf and the King Jackal and the Indian Wolf. The dogs of ancient Egypt were likely domesticated subspecies of one or more of these enigmatic species.

Source (edited): "http://en.wikipedia.org/wiki/Wepwawet"

Werewolf

An 18th century engraving of a werewolf

A **werewolf**, also known as a **lycanthrope** (from the Greek λυκάνθρωπος: λύκος, *lukos*, "wolf", and ἄνθρωπος, *anthrōpos*, man), is a mythological or folkloric human with the ability to shapeshift into a wolf or an anthropomorphic wolf-like creature, either purposely, by being bitten by another werewolf, or after being placed under a curse. This transformation is often associated with the appearance of the full moon, as popularly noted by the medieval chronicler Gervase of Tilbury, and perhaps in earlier times among the ancient Greeks through the writings of Petronius.

Werewolves are often attributed superhuman strength and senses, far beyond those of both wolves and men.

The werewolf is generally held as a European character, although its lore spread through the world in later times. Shape-shifters, similar to werewolves, are common in tales from all over the world, most notably amongst the Native Americans, though most of them involve animal forms other than wolves.

Werewolves are a frequent subject of modern fictional books, although fictional werewolves have been attributed traits distinct from those of original folklore, most notably vulnerability to silver bullets. Werewolves continue to endure in modern culture and fiction, with books, films and television shows cementing the werewolf's stance as a dominant figure in horror.

Etymology

The word *werewolf* is thought to derive from Old English *wer* (or *were*)— pronounced variously as /ˈwɛər, ˈwɪər, ˈwɜr/— and *wulf*. The first part, *wer*, translates as "man" (in the specific sense of male human, not the race of humanity generally). It has cognates in several Germanic languages including Gothic *wair*, Old High German *wer*, and Old Norse *verr*, as well as in other Indo-European languages, such as Sanskrit 'vira', Latin *vir*, Irish *fear*, Lithuanian *vyras*, and Welsh *gŵr*, which have the same meaning. The second half, *wulf*, is the ancestor of modern English "wolf"; in some cases it also had the general meaning "beast."

An alternative etymology derives the first part from Old English *weri* (to wear); the full form in this case would be glossed as *wearer of wolf skin*. Related to this interpretation is Old Norse *ulfhednar*, which denoted lupine equivalents of the *berserker*, said to wear a bearskin in battle.

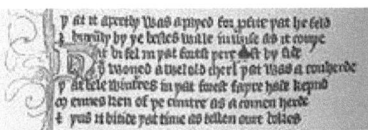

Facsimile of the first seven lines of the 14th century English translation of the 12th century French manuscript *The Romance of William of Palerne*

Yet other sources derive the word from *warg-wolf*, where *warg* (or later *werg* and *wero*) is cognate with Old Norse *vargr*, meaning "rogue," "outlaw," or, euphemistically, "wolf". A *Vargulf* was the kind of wolf that slaughtered many members of a flock or herd but ate little of the kill. This was a serious problem for herders, who had to somehow destroy the rogue wolf before it destroyed the entire flock or herd. The term *Warg* was used in Old English for this kind of wolf. Possibly related is the fact that, in Norse society, an outlaw (who could be murdered with no legal repercussions and was forbidden to receive aid) was typically called *vargr*.

Other terms

The term *lycanthropy*, referring both to the ability to transform oneself into a wolf and to the act of so doing, comes from Ancient Greek *lykánthropos* (λυκάνθρωπος): λύκος, *lýkos* ("wolf") + ἄνθρωπος, *ánthrōpos* ("human").

A compound of which "lyc-" derives from the Proto-Indo-European root *wlkwo-*, meaning "wolf", formally denotes the "wolf - man" transformation. Lycanthropy is but one form of therianthropy, the ability to metamorphose into animals in general. The term *therianthrope* literally means "beast-man."

The word has also been linked to the original werewolf of classical mythology, Lycaon, a king of Arcadia who, according to Ovid's *Metamorphoses*, was turned into a ravenous wolf in retribution for attempting to serve his own son to visiting Zeus in an attempt to disprove the god's divinity.

There is also a mental illness called lycanthropy in which a patient believes he or she is, or has transformed into, an animal and behaves accordingly. This is sometimes referred to as clinical lycanthropy to distinguish it from its use in legends. Despite its origin as a term for man-wolf transformations only, lycanthropy is used in this sense for animals of any type. This broader meaning is often used in modern fictional references, such as in roleplaying game culture.

Another ancient term for shapeshifting between any animal forms is *versipellis*, from which the English words *turnskin* and *turncoat* are derived. This Latin word is similar in meaning to words used for werewolves and other shapeshifters in Russian (*oboroten*) and Old Norse (*hamrammr*).

The French name for a werewolf, sometimes used in English, is *loup-garou* (pronounced /luga'ru/), from the Latin noun lupus meaning wolf. The second element is thought to be from Old French *garoul* meaning "werewolf." This in turn is most likely from Frankish **wer-wulf* meaning "man-wolf."

History of western werewolves

Classical literature

Zeus turning Lycaon into a wolf, engraving by Hendrik Goltzius.

A few references to men changing into wolves are found in Ancient Greek literature and mythology. Herodotus, in his *Histories*, wrote that the Neuri, a tribe he places to the north-east of Scythia, were all transformed into wolves once every year for several days, and then changed back to their human shape. In the second century BC, the Greek geographer Pausanius relates the story of Lycaon, who was transformed into a wolf because he had ritually murdered a child. In accounts by Apollodorus (or pseudo-Apollodorus, *Bibliotheca* 3.8.1) and Ovid (*Metamorphoses* I.219-239), Lycaon serves human flesh to Zeus, wanting to know if he is really a god. Lycaon's transformation, therefore, is punishment for a crime, considered variously as murder, cannibalism, and impiety. Ovid also relates stories of men who roamed the woods of Arcadia in the form of wolves.

Besides Ovid, other Roman writers also treated lycanthropy. Virgil wrote of human beings transforming into wolves. Pliny the Elder relates two tales of lycanthropy. Quoting Euanthes, he mentions a man who hung his clothes on an ash tree and swam across an Arcadian lake, transforming him into a wolf. On the condition that he attacked no human being for nine years, he would be free to swim back across the lake to resume human form. Pliny also quotes Agriopas regarding a tale of a man who was turned into a wolf after tasting the entrails of a human child.

In the Latin work of prose, the *Satyricon*, written about 60 C.E. by Gaius Petronius Arbiter, one of the characters, Niceros, tells a story at a banquet about a friend who turned into a wolf (chs. 61-62). He describes the incident as follows, "When I look for my buddy I see he'd stripped and piled his clothes by the roadside...He pees in a circle round his clothes and then, just like that, turns into a wolf!...after he turned into a wolf he started howling and then ran off into the woods."

Folk beliefs

Description and common attributes

Werewolves were said in European folklore to bear tell-tale physical traits even in their human form. These included the meeting of both eyebrows at the bridge of the nose, curved fingernails, low set ears and a swinging stride. One method of identifying a werewolf in its human form was to cut the flesh of the accused, under the pretense that fur would be seen within the wound. A Russian superstition recalls a werewolf can be recognised by bristles under the tongue. The appearance of a werewolf in its animal form varies from culture to culture, though they are most commonly portrayed as being indistinguishable from ordinary wolves save for the fact that they have no tail (a trait thought characteristic of witches in animal form), are often larger, and retain human eyes and voice. According to some Swedish accounts, the werewolf could be distinguished from a regular wolf by the fact that it would run on three legs, stretching the fourth one backwards to look like a tail. After returning to their human forms, werewolves are usually documented as becoming weak, debilitated and undergoing painful nervous depression. Many historical werewolves were written to have suffered severe melancholia and manic depression, being bitterly conscious of their crimes. One universally reviled trait in medieval Europe was the werewolf's habit of devouring recently buried corpses, a trait that is documented extensively, particularly in the *Annales Medico-psychologiques* in the 19th century. Fennoscandian werewolves were usually old women who possessed poison coated claws and had the ability to paralyse cattle and children with their gaze. Serbian *vulkodlak*s traditionally had the habit of congregating annually in the winter months, when they would strip off their wolf skins and hang them from trees. They would then get a hold of another *vulkodlak*s skin and burn it, releasing the *vulkodlak* from whom the skin came from its curse. The Haitian *jé-rouges* typically try to trick mothers into giving away their children voluntarily by waking them at night and asking their permission to take their child, to which the disoriented mother may either reply yes or no.

Becoming a werewolf

Various methods for becoming a werewolf have been reported, one of the simplest being the removal of clothing and putting on a belt made of wolfskin, probably as a substitute for the assumption of an entire animal skin (which also is frequently described). In other cases, the body is rubbed with a magic salve. To drink rainwater out of the footprint of the animal in question or to drink from certain enchanted streams were also considered effectual modes of accomplishing metamorphosis. The 16th century Swedish writer Olaus Magnus says that the Livonian werewolves were initiated by draining a cup of specially prepared beer and repeating a set formula. Ralston in his *Songs of the Russian People* gives the form of incantation still familiar in Russia.

In Italy, France and Germany, it was said that a man or woman could turn into a werewolf if he or she, on a certain Wednesday or Friday, slept outside on a summer night with the full moon shining directly on his face.

In other cases, the transformation was supposedly accomplished by Satanic allegiance for the most loathsome ends, often for the sake of sating a craving for human flesh. "The werewolves", writes Richard Verstegan (*Restitution of Decayed Intelligence*, 1628), are certayne sorcerers, who having annoynted their bodies with an ointment which they make by the instinct of the devil, and putting on a certayne inchaunted girdle, does not only unto the view of others seem as wolves, but to their own thinking have both the shape and nature of wolves, so long as they wear the said girdle. And they do dispose themselves as very wolves, in worrying and killing, and most of humane creatures.

Such were the views about lycanthropy current throughout the continent of Europe when Verstegan wrote.

The phenomenon of repercussion, the power of animal metamorphosis, or of sending out a familiar, real or spiritual, as a messenger, and the supernormal powers conferred by association with such a familiar, are also attributed to the magician, male and female, all the world over; and witch superstitions are closely parallel to, if not identical with, lycanthropic beliefs, the occasional involuntary character of lycanthropy being almost the sole distinguishing feature. In another direction the phenomenon of repercussion is asserted to manifest itself in connection with the bush-soul of the West African and the *nagual* of Central America; but though there is no line of demarcation to be drawn on logical grounds, the assumed power of the magician and the intimate association of the bush-soul or the *nagual* with a human being are not termed lycanthropy. Nevertheless it will be well to touch on both these beliefs here.

The curse of lycanthropy was also considered by some scholars as being a divine punishment. Werewolf literature shows many examples of God or saints allegedly cursing those who invoked their wrath with werewolfism. Those who were excommunicated by the Roman Catholic Church were also said to become werewolves.

The power of transforming others into wild beasts was attributed not only to malignant sorcerers, but to Christian saints as well. *Omnes angeli, boni et Mali, ex virtute naturali habent potestatem transmutandi corpora nostra* ("All angels, good and bad have the power of transmutating our bodies") was the dictum of St. Thomas Aquinas. St. Patrick was said to have transformed the Welsh king Vereticus into a wolf; Natalis supposedly cursed an illustrious Irish family whose members were each doomed to be a wolf for seven years. In other tales the divine agency is even more direct, while in Russia, again, men supposedly became werewolves when incurring the wrath of the Devil.

A notable exception to the association of Lycanthropy and the Devil, comes from a rare and lesser known account of an 80-year-old man named Thiess. In 1692, in Jurgenburg, Livonia, Thiess testified under oath that he and other werewolves were the Hounds of God. He claimed they were warriors who went down into hell to do battle with witches and demons. Their efforts ensured that the Devil and his minions did not carry off the grain from local failed crops down to hell. Thiess was steadfast in his assertions, claiming that werewolves in Germany and Russia also did battle with the devil's minions in their own versions of hell, and insisted that when werewolves died, their souls were welcomed into heaven as reward for their service. Thiess was ultimately sentenced to ten lashes for Idolatry and superstitious belief.

A distinction is often made between voluntary and involuntary werewolves. The former are generally thought to have made a pact, usually with the Devil, and morph into werewolves at night to indulge in nefarious acts. Involuntary werewolves, on the other hand, are werewolves by an accident of birth or health. In some cultures, individuals born during a new moon or suffering from epilepsy were considered likely to be werewolves.

Becoming a werewolf simply by being bitten by another werewolf as a form of contagion is common in modern horror fiction, but this kind of transmission is rare in legend, unlike the case in vampirism.

Even if the denotation of lycanthropy is limited to the wolf-metamorphosis of living human beings, the beliefs classed together under this head are far from uniform, and the term is somewhat capriciously applied. The transformation may be temporary or permanent; the were-animal may be the man himself metamorphosed; may be his double whose activity leaves the real man to all appearance unchanged; may be his soul, which goes forth seeking whom it may devour, leaving its body in a state of trance; or it may be no more than the messenger of the human being, a real animal or a familiar spirit, whose intimate connection with its owner is shown by the fact that any injury to it is believed, by a phenomenon known as repercussion, to cause a corresponding injury to the human being.

Vulnerabilities

Most modern fiction describes werewolves as vulnerable to silver weapons and highly resistant to other injuries. This feature does not appear in stories about werewolves before the 19th century. (The claim that the Beast of Gévaudan, an 18th century wolf or wolf-like creature, was shot by a silver bullet appears to have been introduced by novelists retelling the story from 1935 onwards and not in earlier versions.)

Unlike vampires, they are not generally thought to be harmed by religious artifacts such as crucifixes and holy water. In many countries, rye and mistletoe were considered effective safeguards against werewolf attacks. Mountain ash is also considered effective, with one Belgian superstition stating that no house was safe unless under the shade of a mountain ash. In some legends, werewolves have an aversion to wolfsbane.

Remedies

Various methods have existed for removing the werewolf form. In antiquity, the Ancient Greeks and Romans believed in the power of exhaustion in curing people of lycanthropy. The victim would be subjected to long periods of physical activity in the hope of being purged of the malady. This practice stemmed from the fact that many alleged werewolves would be left feeling weak and debilitated after committing depredations.

In medieval Europe, traditionally, there are three methods one can use to cure a victim of werewolfism; medicinally (usually via the use of wolfsbane), surgically or by exorcism. However, many of the cures advocated by medieval medical practitioners proved fatal to the patients. A Sicilian belief of Arabic origin holds that a werewolf can be cured of its ailment by striking it on the forehead or scalp with a knife. Another belief from the same culture involves the piercing of the werewolf's hands with nails. Sometimes, less extreme methods were used. In the German lowland of Schleswig-Holstein, a werewolf could be cured if one were to simply address it three times by its Christian name, while one Danish belief holds that simply scolding a werewolf will cure it. Conversion to Christianity is also a common method of removing werewolfism in the medieval period. A devotion to St. Hubert has also been cited as both cure for and protection from lycanthropes.

European cultures

Many European countries and cultures influenced by them have stories of werewolves, including Albania (*oik*), Armenia (*mardagayl*), Croatia/Bosnia and Herzegovina (*vukodlak*), France (*loup-garou*), Greece (λυκανθρωπος - *lycanthropos*), Spain (*hombre lobo*), Bulgaria (върколак - *varkolak*), Turkey (*kurtadam*), Czech Republic (*vlkodlak*), Slovakia (*vlkolak*), Serbia/Montenegro (вукодлак - *vukodlak*), Belarus (ваўкалак - *vaukalak*), Russia (оборотень - *oboroten'*), Ukraine (вовкулака - *vovkulaka* and перевертень - *pereverten'*), Poland (*wilkołak*), Romania (*vârcolac, priculici*), Macedonia (*vrkolak*), Slovenia (*volkodlak*), Scotland (*werewolf, wulver*), England (*werewolf*), Ireland (*faoladh* or *conriocht*), Wales (*bleiddddyn*), Germany (*Werwolf*), the Netherlands (*weerwolf*), Denmark/Sweden/Norway (*Varulv*), Norway/Iceland (*kveld-ulf, varúlfur*), Galicia (*lobishome*), Portugal/Brazil (*lobisomem*), Lithuania (*vilkolakis* and *vilkatlakis*), Latvia (*vilkatis* and *vilkacis*), Andorra/Catalonia (*home llop*), Hungary (*Vérfarkas* and *Farkasember*), Estonia (*libahunt*), Finland (*ihmissusi* and *vironsusi*), and Italy (*lupo mannaro*). In northern Europe, there are also tales about people changing into animals including bears, as well as wolves.

A German woodcut from 1722

Werewolves in European tradition were mostly evil men who terrorized people in the form of wolves on command of the Devil, though there were rare narratives of people being transformed involuntarily. In the 10th century, they were given the binomial name of *melancholia canina* and in the 14th century, *daemonium lupum*. In Marie de France's poem *Bisclavret* (c. 1200), the nobleman Bizuneh, for reasons not described in the lai, had to transform into a wolf every week. When his treacherous wife stole his clothing needed to restore his human form, he escaped the king's wolf hunt by imploring the king for mercy and accompanied the king thereafter. His behaviour at court was so much gentler than when his wife and her new husband appeared at court, that his hateful attack on the couple was deemed justly motivated, and the truth was revealed. Other tales of this sort include German fairy tales, *Märchen*, in which several aristocrats temporarily transform into beasts. See *Snow White and Rose Red*, where the tame bear is really a bewitched prince, and *The Golden Bird* where the talking fox is also a man.

Werewolf folklore is rare in England, possibly because wolves had been eradicated by authorities in the Anglo-Saxon period.

Harald I of Norway is known to have had a body of *Úlfhednar* (wolf coated), which are mentioned in Vatnsdœla saga, Haraldskvæði, and the Völsunga saga resemble some werewolf legends. The Úlfhednar were fighters similar to the berserkers, though they dressed in wolf hides rather than those of bears and were reputed to channel the spirits of these animals to enhance effectiveness in battle. These warriors were resistant to pain and killed viciously in battle, much like wild animals. Ulfhednar and berserkers are closely associated with the Norse god Odin.

In Latvian folklore, a vilkacis was someone who transformed into a wolf-like monster, which could be benevolent at times. Another collection of stories concern the skin-walkers. The vilkacis and skin-walkers probably have a common origin in Proto-Indo-European society, where a class of young unwed warriors were apparently associated with wolves.

In Hungarian folklore, the concept of werewolf goes back to the Middle Ages. The werewolves used to live specially in the region of Transdanubia, and it was thought that the ability to change into a wolf was obtained in the infant age, after the suffering of abuse by the parents or by a curse. At the age of seven the boy or the girl leaves the house and goes hunting by night and can change to person or wolf whenever he wants. The curse can also be obtained when in the adulthood the person passed three times through an arch made of a Birch with the help of a wild rose's spine.

The werewolves were known to exterminate all kind of farm animals, especially sheep. The transformation usually occurred in the Winter solstice, Easter and full moon. Later in the XVII and XVIII century, the trials in Hungary not only were conduced against witches, but against werewolves too, and many records exist creating connections between both kinds. Also the vampires and werewolves are closely related in Hungary, being both feared in the antiquity.

According to the first dictionary of modern Serbian language (published by Vuk Stefanović-Karadžić in 1818) *vukodlak / вукодлак* (werewolf) and *vampir / вампир* (vampire) are synonyms, meaning a man who returns from his grave for purposes of fornicating with his widow. The dictionary states this to be a common folk tale.

Common among the Kashubs of what is now northern Poland, and the Serbs and Slovenes, was the belief that if a child was born with hair, a birthmark or a caul on their head, they were supposed to possess shape-shifting abilities. Though capable of turning into any animal they wished, it was commonly believed that such people preferred to turn into a wolf.

According to Armenian lore, there are women who, in consequence of deadly sins, are condemned to spend seven years in wolf form. In a typical account, a condemned woman is visited by a wolfskin-toting spirit, who orders her to wear the skin, which causes her to acquire frightful cravings for human flesh soon after. With her better nature overcome, the she-wolf devours each of her own children, then her relatives' children in order of relationship, and finally the children of strangers. She wanders only at night, with doors and locks springing open at her approach. When morning arrives, she reverts to human form and removes her wolfskin. The transformation is generally said to be involuntary, but there are alternate versions involving voluntary metamorphosis, where the women can transform at will.

The 11th Century Belarusian Prince Usiaslau of Polatsk was considered to have been a Werewolf, capable of moving at superhuman speeds, as recounted in *The Tale of Igor's Campaign*: "Vseslav the prince judged men; as prince, he ruled towns; but at night he prowled in the guise of a wolf. From Kiev, prowling, he reached, before the cocks crew, Tmutorokan. The path of Great Sun, as a wolf, prowling, he crossed. For him in Polotsk they rang for matins early at St. Sophia the bells; but he heard the ringing in Kiev."

There were numerous reports of werewolf attacks – and consequent court trials – in 16th century France. In some of the cases there was clear evidence against the accused of murder and cannibalism, but none of association with wolves; in other cases people have been terrified by such creatures, such as that of Gilles Garnier in Dole in 1573, there was clear evidence against some wolf but none against the accused. The *loup-garou* eventually ceased to be regarded as a dangerous heretic and reverted to the pre-Christian notion of a "man-wolf-fiend." The *lubins* or *lupins* were usually female and shy in contrast to the aggressive *loups-garous*.

Some French werewolf lore is associated with documented events. The Beast of Gévaudan terrorized the general area of the former province of Gévaudan, now called Lozère, in south-central France. From the years 1764 to 1767, an unknown entity killed upwards of 80 men, women, and children. The creature was described as a giant wolf by the sole survivor of the attacks, which ceased after several wolves were killed in the area.

At the beginning of the 17th century witchcraft was prosecuted by James I of England, who regarded "warwoolfes" as victims of delusion induced by "a natural superabundance of melancholic."

American cultures

During the Norse colonization of the Americas, it is thought by Woodward that the Vikings brought with them their beliefs in werewolves, which would manifest themselves in the folklore of some Native American tribes.

The Naskapis believed that the caribou afterlife is guarded by giant wolves which kill careless hunters venturing too near. The Navajo people feared witches in wolf's clothing called "Maicob".

When the European colonization of the Americas occurred, the pioneers brought their own werewolf folklore with them and were later influenced by the lore of their neighbouring colonies and those of the Natives. Belief in the *loup-garou* present in Canada, the Upper and Lower Peninsulas of Michigan and upstate New York, originates from French folklore influenced by Native American stories on the Wendigo. In Mexico, there is a belief in a creature called the *nahual*, which traditionally limits itself to stealing cheese and raping women rather than murder. In Haiti, there is a superstition that werewolf spirits known locally as *Jé-rouge* (red eyes) can possess the bodies of unwitting persons and nightly transform them into cannibalistic lupine creatures.

Asian cultures

Common Turkic folklore holds a different, reverential light to the werewolf legends in that Turkic Central Asian shamans after performing long and arduous rites would voluntarily be able to transform into the humanoid "Kurtadam" (literally meaning Wolfman). Since the wolf was the totemic ancestor animal of the Turkic peoples, they would be respectful of any shaman who was in such a form.

Origins of werewolf beliefs

Many authors have speculated that werewolf legends may have been used to explain serial killings.. This theory is given credence by the tendency of some modern serial killers to indulge in practices commonly associated with werewolves, such as cannibalism, mutilation, and cyclic attacks. The idea is well explored in Sabine Baring-Gould's work *The Book of Werewolves*.

Until the 20th century, wolf attacks on humans were an occasional, but widespread feature of life in Europe. Some scholars have suggested that it was inevitable that wolves, being the most feared predators in Europe, were projected into the folklore of evil shapeshifters. This is said to be corroborated by the fact that areas devoid of wolves typically use different kinds of predator to fill the niche; *werehyenas* in Africa, *weretigers* in India, as well as *werepumas* ("runa uturuncu") and *werejaguars* ("yaguaraté-abá" or "tigre-capiango") of southern South America.

In his *Man into Wolf* (1948), anthropologist Robert Eisler drew attention to the fact that many Indo-European tribal names and some modern European surnames mean "wolf" or "wolf-men". This is argued by Eisler to indicate that the European transition from fruit gathering to predatory hunting was a conscious process, simultaneously accompanied by an emotional upheaval still remembered in humanity's subconscious, which in turn became reflected in the later medieval superstition of werewolves.

Werewolf, by Lucas Cranach der Ältere, 1512

Some modern researchers have tried to explain the reports of werewolf behaviour with recognised medical conditions. Dr Lee Illis of Guy's Hospital in London wrote a paper in 1963 entitled *On Porphyria and the Aetiology of Werewolves*, in which he argues that historical accounts on werewolves could have in fact been referring to victims of congenital porphyria, stating how the symptoms of photosensitivity, reddish teeth and psychosis could have been grounds for accusing a sufferer of being a werewolf. This is however argued against by Woodward, who points out how mythological werewolves were almost invariably portrayed as resembling true wolves, and that their human forms were rarely physically conspicuous as porphyria victims. Others have pointed out the possibility of historical werewolves having been sufferers of hypertrichosis, a hereditary condition manifesting itself in excessive hair growth. However, Woodward dismissed the possibility, as the rarity of the disease ruled it out from happening on a large scale, as werewolf cases were in medieval Europe. People suffering from Down's Syndrome have been suggested by some scholars to have been possible originators of werewolf myths. Woodward suggested rabies as the origin of werewolf beliefs, claiming remarkable similarities between the symptoms of that disease and some of the legends. Woodward focused on the idea that being bitten by a werewolf could result in the victim turning into one, which suggested the idea of a transmittable disease like rabies. However, the idea that lycanthropy could be transmitted in this way is not part of the original myths and legends and only appears in relatively recent beliefs.

Vampiric connections

In Medieval Europe, the corpses of some people executed as werewolves were cremated rather than buried in order to prevent them from being resurrected as vampires. Before the end of the 19th century, the Greeks believed that the corpses of werewolves, if not destroyed, would return to life as vampires in the form of wolves or hyenas which prowled battlefields, drinking the blood of dying soldiers. In the same vein, in some rural areas of Germany, Poland and Northern France, it was once believed that people who died in mortal sin came back to life as blood-drinking wolves. This differs from conventional werewolfery, where the creature is a living being rather than an undead apparition. These vampiric werewolves would return to their human corpse form at daylight. They were dealt with by decapitation with a spade and exorcism by the parish priest. The head would then be thrown into a stream, where the weight of its sins were thought to weigh it down. Sometimes, the same methods used to dispose of ordinary vampires would be used. The vampire was also linked to the werewolf in East European countries, particularly Bulgaria, Serbia and Slovenia. In Serbia, the werewolf and vampire are known collectively as one creature; *Vulkodlak*. In Hungarian and Balkan mythology, many werewolves were said to be vampiric witches who became wolves in order to suck the blood of men born under the full moon in order to preserve their health. In their human form, these werewolves were said to have pale, sunken faces, hollow eyes, swollen lips and flabby arms. The Haitian *jé-rouges* differ from traditional

European werewolves by their habit of actively trying to spread their lycanthropic condition to others, much like vampires.

In fiction

The first feature film to use an anthropomorphic werewolf was *Werewolf of London* in 1935. The main werewolf of this film is a dapper London scientist who retains some of his style and most of his human features after his transformation, as lead actor Henry Hull was unwilling to spend long hours being made up by makeup artist Jack Pierce. Universal Studios drew on a Balkan tale of a plant associated with lycanthropy as there was no literary work to draw upon, unlike the case with vampires. There is no reference to silver nor other aspects of werewolf lore such as cannibalism.

A more tragic character is Talbot, played by Lon Chaney, Jr. in 1941's *The Wolf Man*. With Pierce's makeup more elaborate this time, the movie catapulted the werewolf into public consciousness. Sympathetic portrayals are few but notable, such as the comedic but tortured protagonist David Naughton in *An American Werewolf in London*, and a less anguished and more confident and charismatic Jack Nicholson in the 1994 film *Wolf*. Rachel Hawthorne's *Dark Guardian* novels examine a secret society of werewolves who live peacefully alongside normal humans, are able to initiate the change at will to protect their kind, and generally retain control of themselves when transformed. Other werewolves are decidedly more willful and malevolent, such as those in the novel *The Howling* and its subsequent sequels and film adaptations. The form a werewolf assumes was generally anthropomorphic in early films such as *The Wolf Man* and *Werewolf of London*, but larger and powerful wolf in many later films.

Werewolves are often depicted as immune to damage caused by ordinary weapons, being vulnerable only to silver objects, such as a silver-tipped cane, bullet or blade; this attribute was first adopted cinematically in *The Wolf Man*. This negative reaction to silver is sometimes so strong that the mere touch of the metal on a werewolf's skin will cause burns. Current-day werewolf fiction almost exclusively involves lycanthropy being either a hereditary condition or being transmitted like an infectious disease by the bite of another werewolf. In some fiction, the power of the werewolf extends to human form, such as invulnerability, super-human speed and strength and falling on their feet from high falls. Also aggressiveness and animalistic urges may be harder to control (hunger, sexual arousal). Usually in these cases the abilities are diminished in human form. In other fictions, it can even be cured by medicine men or even antidotes.

Fantastic literature sometimes includes the painful element to the change, but often does not. For example, J. K. Rowling maintains the painful transition between forms while Charles de Lint, Terry Pratchett, Fritz Leiber, and myriad others reach back to the non-painful medieval literary sources. Poul Anderson in *Operation Chaos* presents a modernised American werewolf, in complete control of himself and free of the traditional taints, while in *Three Hearts and Three Lions* appears a far more traditional (though not unsympathetic) female werewolf.
Source (edited): "http://en.wikipedia.org/wiki/Werewolf"

Werewolf witch trials

Werewolf, by Lucas Cranach der Ältere, 1512

The **Werewolf witch trials** were witch trials combined with werewolf trials. These largely took place in the Baltic countries, especially in Estonia, where the witch trials, affected by the belief in werewolves in the area, looked different than in other countries.

The Werewolf witch trials of Estonia

In Estonia, around one hundred witch trials were held in 1610-1650, and 29 women and 26 men are recorded executed for sorcery. A book about witchcraft was published in Riga in 1626. Christianity had been established by the end of the 13th century in Estonia, but ceremonies which had a pagan origin were common in the following centuries. As in much of Europe in the 17th century, an interest in the occult and the supernatural was popular, and the belief in werewolves common, and the Baltic witch trials were therefore more or less werewolf trials: the public regarded the accused as werewolves, while the authorities judged them as witches.

Accusations of magic, which were often about enchanted potions, were rare in Estonia; the belief in magic was common, but it was not associated with the Devil, rather it was considered a skill which could be inherited or cultivated. Accusations of werewolves, on the other hand, were common. At 18 trials, 18 women and 13 men were accused for damage on property and cattle they had caused in the shape of werewolves. Under torture, they confessed having hidden their wolves skin under a rock. The only thing needed to make this a witch trial was a pact with the

Devil. This confession was extracted from the accused by use of torture. The authorities aim was to make people associated magic and Pagan customs with the Devil and coordinate them with the belief of the Protestant church, as the Catholic Church in Balticum had not succeeded with this.

The werewolf was not always regarded as evil. A notable case in Jürgensburg in Livonia in 1692, follows a similar pattern, but did not end in a death sentence: the eighty year old Thiess confessed to be a werewolf who, with other werewolves, regularly went to hell three times a year to fight the witches and wizards of Satan to ensure a good harvest. This case is also notable because this description is similar to the Benandanti. The court tried to make Thiess confess that he had made a pact with the Devil and that the werewolf was in the service of Satan, but they did not succeed, and he was sentenced to whipping on 10 October 1692. The werewolf trials petered out at the end of the 17th century. As late as 1696, however, a pack of werewolves was believed to run wild in Vastemoisa under their leader Libbe Matz. The last trial of sorcery was performed in Harju County in 1816, when the farmer Jacob and his spouse Anna, along with four others, were accused of trying to track thieves by use of magic: it ended in the whipping of Jacob and Anna and the rest being reprimanded for "fraud which appeals to superstitions and ignorance".

Hans the Werewolf

The so called "Hans the Werewolf" was allegedly an Estonian werewolf and witch. His trial is a typical example of the combined werewolf and witch trials, which dominated witch hunts in Estonia.

In 1651, Hans was brought before the court in Idavare accused of being a werewolf at the age of eighteen. He had confessed that he had hunted as a werewolf for two years. "When asked by the judges if his body took part in the hunt, or if only his soul was transmuted, Hans confirmed that he had found a dog's teeth-marks on his own leg, which he had received while a werewolf. Further asked whether he felt himself to be a man or a beast while transmuted, he said that he felt himself to be beast"

He claimed he had gotten the body of a wolf by a man in black. The court asked if it was his soul or his body participating when he turned into a werewolf and if he felt as an animal or a human when he did. He answered that he felt like a wild beast. Thereby, the court considered it proved that he had not dressed out, but really transformed into a werewolf, which meant he had undergone a magical transformation. Furthermore, as he was given this disguise by a "man in black," which the court thought was obviously Satan, he could be judged guilty of witchcraft and sentenced to death. In the Baltic countries, this was a common method of turning a werewolf trial into a witch trial.

Source (edited): "http://en.wikipedia.org/wiki/Werewolf_witch_trials"

Wulver

The **wulver** is a kind of werewolf that is exclusively part of the folklore of the Shetland Islands of Scotland. The wulver kept to itself and was not aggressive if left in peace. Unlike most 'werewolves' the Wulver is not a shapeshifter and is not nor was it ever a human being. It appears to be a sort of immortal spirit. Jessie Saxby, in Shetland Traditional Lore (Chapter 9), writes, "The Wulver was a creature like a man with a wolf's head. He had short brown hair all over him. His home was a cave dug out of the side of a steep knowe, halfway up a hill. He didn't molest folk if folk didn't molest him. He was fond of fishing, and had a small rock in the deep water which is known to this day as the 'Wulver's Stane'. There he would sit fishing sillaks and piltaks for hour after hour. He was reported to have frequently left a few fish on the window-sill of some poor body."

A similar un-hostile werewolf is the Faoladh from Irish folklore. The Faoladh was said to protect children and stand guard over wounded men.

Source (edited): "http://en.wikipedia.org/wiki/Wulver"

Fenrir

Odin and Fenris (1909) by Dorothy Hardy

In Norse mythology, **Fenrir** (Old Norse: "fen-dweller"), **Fenrisúlfr** (Old Norse: "Fenris wolf"), **Hróðvitnir** (Old Norse: "fame-wolf"), or **Vánagandr** (Old Norse: "the monster of the river Ván") is a monstrous wolf. Fenrir is attested in the *Poetic Edda*, compiled in the 13th century from earlier traditional sources, and the *Prose Edda* and *Heimskringla*, written in the 13th century by Snorri Sturluson. In both the *Poetic Edda* and *Prose Edda*, Fenrir is the father of the wolves Sköll and Hati Hróðvitnisson, is a son of Loki, and is foretold to kill the god Odin during the events of Ragnarök, but will in turn be killed by Odin's son Víðarr.

In the *Prose Edda*, additional information is given about Fenrir, including that, due to the gods' knowledge of prophecies foretelling great trouble from Fenrir and his rapid growth, the gods bound him, and as a result Fenrir bit off the right hand of the god Týr. Depictions of Fenrir have been identified on various objects, and scholarly theories have been proposed regarding Fenrir's relation to other canine beings in Norse mythology. Fenrir has been the subject of artistic depictions, and he appears in literature.

Attestations

Poetic Edda

Fenrir and Odin (1895) by Lorenz Frølich

An illustration of Víðarr stabbing Fenrir while holding his jaws apart (1908) by W. G. Collingwood, inspired by the Gosforth Cross

Fenrir is mentioned in three stanzas of the poem *Völuspá*, and in two stanzas of the poem *Vafþrúðnismál*. In stanza 40 of the poem *Völuspá*, a völva divulges to Odin that, in the east, an old woman sat in the forest Járnviðr, "and bred there the broods of Fenrir. There will come from them all one of that number to be a moon-snatcher in troll's skin." Further into the poem, the völva foretells that Odin will be consumed by Fenrir at Ragnarök:

Then is fulfilled Hlín's
second sorrow,
when Óðinn goes
to fight with the wolf,
and Beli's slayer,
bright, against Surtr.
Then shall Frigg's
sweet friend fall.

In the stanza that follows, the völva describes that Odin's "tall child of Triumph's Sire" (Odin's son Víðarr) will then come to "strike at the beast of slaughter," and with his hands, he will drive a sword **onto** the heart of "Hveðrungr's son," avenging the death of his father.

In the first of two stanzas mentioning Fenrir in *Vafþrúðnismál*, Odin poses a question to the wise jötunn Vafþrúðnir: "Much I have travelled, much have I tried out,
much have I tested the Powers;
from where will a sun come into the smooth heaven
when Fenrir has assailed this one?"
In the stanza that follows, Vafþrúðnir responds that Sól (here referred to as *Álfröðull*), will bear a daughter before Fenrir attacks her, and that this daughter shall continue the paths of her deceased mother through the heavens.

Prose Edda

Loki's Brood (1905) by Emil Doepler

Loki's Children (1906) by Lorenz Frølich

Týr and Fenrir (1911) by John Bauer

In the *Prose Edda*, Fenrir is mentioned in three books: *Gylfaginning*, *Skáldskaparmál* and *Háttatal*.

Gylfaginning chapters 13 and 25

In chapter 13 of the *Prose Edda* book *Gylfaginning*, Fenrir is first mentioned in a stanza quoted from *Völuspá*. Fenrir is first mentioned in prose in chapter 25, where the enthroned figure of High tells Gangleri (described as King Gylfi in disguise) about the god Týr. High says that one example of Týr's bravery is that when the Æsir were luring Fenrir (referred to here as *Fenrisúlfr*) to place the fetter Gleipnir on the wolf. Fenrir did not trust that they would let him go until the Æsir placed Týr's hand into Fenrir's mouth as a pledge. As a result, when the Æsir refused to release him, he bit off Týr's hand at a location "now called the wolf-joint" (the wrist), causing Týr to be one-handed and "not considered to be a promoter of settlements between people."

Gylfaginning chapter 34

In chapter 34, High describes Loki, and says that Loki had three children with a female jötunn named Angrboða located in the land of Jötunheimr; Fenrisúlfr, the serpent Jörmungandr, and the female being Hel. High continues that, once the gods found that these three children were being brought up in the land of Jötunheimr, and when the gods "traced prophecies that from these siblings great mischief and disaster would arise for them" the gods expected a lot of trouble from the three children, partially due to the nature of the mother of the children, yet worse so due to the nature of their father.

High says that Odin sent the gods to gather the children and bring them to him. Upon their arrival, Odin threw Jörmungandr into "that deep sea that lies round all lands", and then threw Hel into Niflheim, and bestowed upon her authority over nine worlds. However, the Æsir brought up the wolf "at home", and only Týr had the courage to approach Fenrir, and give Fenrir food. The gods noticed that Fenrir was growing rapidly every day, and since all prophecies foretold that Fenrir was destined to cause them harm, the gods formed a plan. The gods prepared three fetters: The first, greatly strong, was called Leyding. They brought Leyding to Fenrir and suggested that the wolf try his strength with it. Fenrir judged that it was not beyond his strength, and so let the gods do what they wanted with it. At Fenrir's first kick the bind snapped, and Fenrir loosened himself from Leyding. The gods made a second fetter, twice as strong, and named it Dromi. The gods asked Fenrir to try the new fetter, and that should he break this feat of engineering, Fenrir would achieve great fame for his strength. Fenrir considered that the fetter was very strong, yet also that his strength had grown since he broke Leyding, yet that he would have to take some risks if he were to become famous. Fenrir allowed them to place the fetter.

When the Æsir exclaimed that they were ready, Fenrir shook himself, knocked the fetter to ground, strained hard, and kicking with his feet, snapped the fetter – breaking it into pieces that flew far into the distance. High says that, as a result, to "loose from Leyding" or to "strike out of Dromi" have become sayings for when something is achieved with great effort. The Æsir started to fear that they would not be able to bind Fenrir, and so Odin sent Freyr's messenger Skírnir down into the land of Svartálfaheimr to "some dwarfs" and had them make a fetter called Gleipnir. The dwarves constructed Gleipnir from six mythical ingredients. After an exchange between Gangleri and High, High continues that the fetter was smooth and soft as a silken ribbon, yet strong and firm. The messenger brought the ribbon to the Æsir, and they thanked him heartily for completing the task.

The Æsir went out on to the lake Amsvartnir sent for Fenrir to accompany them, and continued to the island Lyngvi (Old Norse "a place overgrown with heather"). The gods showed Fenrir the silken fetter Gleipnir, told him to tear it, stated that it was much stronger than it appeared, passed it among themselves, used their hands to pull it, and yet it did not tear. However, they said that Fenrir would be able to tear it, to which Fenrir replied:

"The Binding of Fenrir" (1908) by George Wright

"It looks to me that with this ribbon as though I will gain no fame from it if I do tear apart such a slender band, but if it is made with art and trickery, then even if it does look thin, this band is not going on my legs."

The Æsir said Fenrir would quickly tear apart a thin silken strip, noting that Fenrir earlier broke great iron binds, and added that if Fenrir wasn't able to break slender Gleipnir then Fenrir is nothing for the gods to fear, and as a result would be freed. Fenrir responded: "If you bind me so that I am unable to release myself, then you will be standing by in such a way that I should have to wait a long time before I got any help from you. I am reluctant to have this band put on me. But rather than that you question my courage, let someone put his hand in my mouth as a pledge that this is done in good faith."

With this statement, all of the Æsir look to one another, finding themselves in a dilemma. Everyone refused to place their hand in Fenrir's mouth until Týr put out his right hand and placed it into the wolf's jaws. When Fenrir kicked, Gleipnir caught tightly, and the more Fenrir struggled, the stronger the band grew. At this, everyone laughed, except Týr, who there lost his right hand. When the gods knew that Fenrir was fully bound, they took a cord called Gelgja (Old Norse "fetter") hanging from Gleipnir, inserted the cord through a large stone slab called Gjöll (Old Norse "scream"), and the gods fastened the stone slab deep into the ground. After, the gods took a great rock called Thviti (Old Norse "hitter, batterer"), and thrust it even further into the ground as an anchoring peg. Fenrir reacted violently; he opened his jaws very widely, and tried to bite the gods. The gods thrust "a certain sword" into Fenrir's mouth, the hilt of the sword on Fenrir's lower gums and the point his upper gums. Fenrir "howled horribly," saliva ran from his mouth, and this saliva formed the river Ván (Old Norse "hope"). There Fenrir will lie until Ragnarök. Gangleri comments that Loki created a "pretty terrible family" though important, and asks why the Æsir did not just kill Fenrir there since they expected great malice from him. High replies that "so greatly did the gods respect their holy places and places of sanctuary that they did not want to defile them with the wolf's blood even though the prophecies say that he will be the death of Odin."

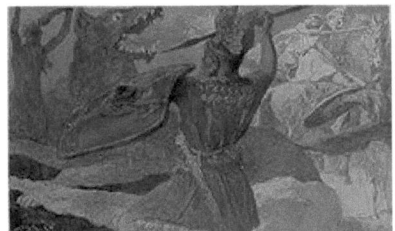

"Odin and Fenriswolf, Freyr and Surt" (1905) by Emil Doepler

Gylfaginning chapters 38 and 51

In chapter 38, High says that there are many men in Valhalla, and many more who will arrive, yet they will "seem too few when the wolf comes." In chapter 51, High foretells that as part of the events of Ragnarök, after Fenrir's son Sköll has swallowed the sun and his other son Hati Hróðvitnisson has swallowed the moon, the stars will disappear from the sky. The earth will shake violently, trees will be uprooted, mountains will fall, and all binds will snap – Fenrisúlfr will be free. Fenrisúlfr will go forth with his mouth opened wide, his upper jaw touching the sky and his lower jaw the earth, and flames will burn from his eyes and nostrils. Later, Fenrisúlfr will arrive at the field Vígríðr with his brother Jörmungandr. With the forces assembled there, an immense battle will take place. During this, Odin will ride to fight Fenrisúlfr. During the battle, Fenrisúlfr will eventually swallow Odin, killing him, and Odin's son Víðarr will move forward and kick one foot into the lower jaw of the wolf. This foot will bear a legendary shoe "for which the material has been collected throughout all time." With one hand, Víðarr will take hold of the wolf's upper jaw and tear apart his mouth, killing Fenrisúlfr. High follows this prose description by citing various quotes from *Völuspá* in support, some of which mention Fenrir.

Fenrir (1874) by A. Fleming

Skáldskaparmál and *Háttatal*

In the Epilogue section of the *Prose Edda* book *Skáldskaparmál*, a euhemerized monologue equates Fenrisúlfr to Pyrrhus, attempting to rationalize that "it killed Odin, and Pyrrhus could be said to be a wolf according to their religion, for he paid no respect to places of sanctuary when he killed the king in the temple in front of Thor's altar." In chapter 2, "wolf's enemy" is cited as a kenning for Odin as used by the 10th century skald Egill Skallagrímsson. In chapter 9, "feeder of the wolf" is given as a kenning for Týr and, in chapter 11, "slayer of Fenrisúlfr" is presented as a kenning for Víðarr. In chapter 50, a section of *Ragnarsdrápa* by the 9th century skald Bragi Boddason is quoted that refers to Hel, the being, as "the monstrous wolf's sister." In chapter 75, names for wargs and wolves are list, including both "Hróðvitnir" and "Fenrir." "Fenrir" appears twice in verse as a common noun for a "wolf" or "warg" in chapter 58 of *Skáldskaparmál*, and in chapter 56 of the book *Háttatal*. Additionally, the name "Fenrir" can be found among a list of jötnar in chapter 75 of *Skáldskaparmál*.

Heimskringla

A 17th century manuscript illustration of the bound Fenrir, the river Ván flowing from his jaws

At the end of the *Heimskringla* saga *Hákonar saga góða*, the poem *Hákonarmál* by the 10th century skald Eyvindr skáldaspillir is presented. The poem is about the fall of King Haakon I of Norway; although he is Christian, he is taken by two valkyries to Valhalla, and is there received as one of the Einherjar. Towards the end of the poem, a stanza relates sooner will the bonds of Fenrir snap than as good a king as Haakon shall stand in his place:
Unfettered will fare the Fenris Wolf
and ravaged the realm of men,
ere that cometh a kingly prince
as good, to stand in his stead.

Archaeological record

Thorwald's Cross at Kirk Andreas, Isle of Man

The Ledberg stone in Sweden

Thorwald's Cross
Thorwald's Cross, a partially surviving runestone erected at Kirk Andreas on the Isle of Man, depicts a bearded human holding a spear downward at a wolf, his right foot in its mouth, while a large bird sits at his shoulder. Rundata dates it to 940, while Pluskowski dates it to the 11th century. This depiction has been interpreted as Odin, with a raven or eagle at his shoulder, being consumed by Fenrir at Ragnarök. On the reverse of the stone is another image parallel to it that has been described as Christ triumphing over Satan. These combined elements have led to the cross as being described as "syncretic art"; a mixture of pagan and Christian beliefs.

Gosforth Cross
The mid-11th century Gosforth Cross, located in Cumbria, England, has been described as depicting a combination of scenes from the Christian Judgement Day and the pagan Ragnarök. The cross features various figures depicted in Borre style, including a man with a spear facing a monstrous head, one of whose feet is thrust into the beast's forked tongue and on its lower jaw, while a hand is placed against its upper jaw, a scene interpreted as Víðarr fighting Fenrir. This depiction has been theorized as a metaphor for Christ's defeat of Satan.

Ledberg stone
The 11th century Ledberg stone in Sweden, similarly to Thorwald's Cross, features a figure with his foot at the mouth of a four-legged beast, and this may also be a depiction of Odin being devoured by Fenrir at Ragnarök. Below the beast and the man is a depiction of a legless, helmeted man, with his arms in a prostrate position. The Younger Futhark inscription on the stone bears a commonly seen memorial dedication, but is followed by an encoded runic sequence that has been described as "mysterious," and "an interesting magic formula which is known from all over the ancient Norse world."

Other
If the images on the Tullstorp Runestone are correctly identified as depicting Ragnarök, then Fenrir is shown above the ship Naglfar.

Meyer Schapiro theorizes a connection between the "Hell Mouth" that appears in medieval Christian iconography and Fenrir. According to Schapiro, "the Anglo-Saxon taste for the Hell Mouth was perhaps influenced by the northern pagan myth of the Crack of Doom and the battle with the wolf, who devoured Odin."

Theories

Fenrir bites off the hand of a sword-wielding Týr in an illustration on an 18th century Icelandic manuscript

In reference to Fenrir's presentation in the *Prose Edda*, Andy Orchard theorizes that "the hound (or wolf)" Garmr, Sköll, and Hati Hróðvitnisson were originally simply all Fenrir, stating that "Snorri, characteristically, is careful to make distinctions, naming the wolves who devour the sun and moon as Sköll and Hati Hróðvitnisson respectively, and describing an encounter between Garm and Týr (who, one would have thought, might like to get his hand on Fenrir) at Ragnarök."

John Lindow says that it is unclear why the gods decide to raise Fenrir as opposed to his siblings Hel and Jörmungandr in *Gylfaginning* chapter 35, theorizing that it may be "because Odin had a connection with wolves? Because Loki was Odin's blood brother?" Referring to the same chapter, Lindow comments that neither of the phrases that Fenrir's binding result in have left any other traces. Lindow compares Fenrir's role to his father Loki and Fenrir's brother Jörmungandr, in that they all spend time with the gods, are bound or cast out by them, return "at the end of the current mythic order to destroy them, only to be destroyed himself as a younger generation of gods, one of them his slayer, survives into the new world order."

Indo-European parallels have been proposed between myths of Fenrir and the Persian demon Ahriman. The Yashts refer to a story where Taxma Urupi rode Angra Mainyu as a horse for thirty years. An elaboration of this allusion is found only in a late Parsi commentary. The ruler Taxmoruw (Taxma Urupi) managed to lasso Ahriman (Angra Mainyu) and keep him tied up while taking him for a ride three times a day. After thirty years Ahriman outwitted and swallowed Taxmoruw. In a sexual encounter with Ahriman, Jamshid, Taxmoruw's brother, inserted his hand into Ahriman's anus and pulled out his brother's corpse. His hand withered from contact with the diabolic innards. The suggested parallels with Fenrir myths are the binding of an evil being by a ruler figure and the subsequent swallowing of the ruler figure by the evil being (Odin and Fenrir), trickery involving the thrusting of a hand into a monster's orifice and the affliction of the inserted limb (Týr and Fenrir).

Ethologist Dr. Valerius Geist of the University of Calgary, Alberta wrote that Fenrir's maiming and ultimate killing of Odin, who had previously nurtured him, was likely based on true experiences of wolf-behaviour, seeing as wolves are genetically encoded to rise up the pack hierarchy and have on occasion been recorded to rebel against and kill their parents. Geist states that "apparently, even the ancients knew that wolves may turn on their parents and siblings and kill them."

Modern influence

Fenrir has been depicted in the artwork "Odin and Fenris" (1909) and "The Binding of Fenris" (around 1900) by Dorothy Hardy, "Odin und Fenriswolf" and "Fesselung des Fenriswolfe" (1901) by Emil Doepler, and is the subject of the metal sculpture "Fenrir" by A. V. Gunnerud located on the island of Askøy, Norway.

Fenrir appears in modern literature in the poem "Om Fenrisulven og Tyr" (1819) by Adam Gottlob Oehlenschläger (collected in *Nordens Guder*), the novel *Der Fenriswolf* by K. H. Strobl, and *Til kamp mod dødbideriet* (1974) by E. K. Reich and E. Larsen.

Notes

References

External links

- Media related to Fenrir at Wikimedia Commons

Source (edited): "http://en.wikipedia.org/wiki/Fenrir"

Geri and Freki

The god Odin enthroned and flanked by the wolves Geri and Freki and the ravens Huginn and Muninn as illustrated (1882) by Carl Emil Doepler.

In Norse mythology, **Geri** and **Freki** (Old Norse, both meaning "the ravenous" or "greedy one") are two wolves which are said to accompany the god Odin. They are attested in the *Poetic Edda*, a collection of epic poetry compiled in the 13th century from earlier traditional sources, in the *Prose Edda*, written in the 13th century by Snorri Sturluson, and in the poetry of skalds. The pair has been compared to similar figures found in Greek, Roman and Vedic mythology, and may also be connected to beliefs surrounding the Germanic "wolf-warrior bands", the Úlfhéðnar.

Etymology

The names *Geri* and *Freki* have been interpreted as meaning either "the greedy one" or "the ravenous one". The name *Geri* can be traced back to the Proto-Germanic adjective **geraz*, attested in Burgundian *girs*, Old Norse *gerr* and Old High German *ger* or *giri*, all of which mean "greedy". The name *Freki* can be traced back to the Proto-Germanic adjective **frekaz*, attested in Gothic *faihu-friks* "covetous, avaricious", Old Norse *frekr* "greedy", Old English *frec* "desirous, greedy, gluttonous, audacious" and Old High German *freh* "greedy". John Lindow interprets both Old Norse names as nominalized adjectives. Bruce Lincoln further traces *Geri* back to a Proto-Indo-European stem **gher-*, which is the same as that found in *Garmr*, a name referring to the hound closely associated with the events of Ragnarök.

Attestations

In the *Poetic Edda* poem *Grímnismál*, the god Odin (disguised as *Grímnir*) provides the young Agnarr with information about Odin's companions. Agnarr is told that Odin feeds Geri and Freki while the god himself consumes only wine:
The pair is also alluded to via the kenning "Viðrir's (Odin's) hounds" in *Helgakviða Hundingsbana I*, verse 13, where it is related that they roam the field "greedy for the corpses of those who have fallen in battle".
In the *Prose Edda* book *Gylfaginning* (chapter 38), the enthroned figure of High explains that Odin gives all of the food on his table to his wolves Geri and Freki and that Odin requires no food, for wine is to him both meat and drink. High then quotes the above mentioned stanza from the poem *Grímnismál* in support. In chapter 75 of the *Prose Edda* book *Skáldskaparmál* a list of names for wargs and wolves is provided that includes both Geri and Freki.
In skaldic poetry *Geri* and *Freki* are used as common nouns for "wolf" in chapter 58 of *Skáldskaparmál* (quoted in works by the skalds Þjóðólfr of Hvinir and Egill Skallagrímsson) and *Geri* is again used as a common noun for "wolf" in chapter 64 of the *Prose Edda* book *Háttatal*. Geri is referenced in kennings for "blood" in chapter 58 of *Skáldskaparmál* ("Geri's ales" in a work by the skald Þórðr Sjáreksson) and in for "carrion" in chapter 60 ("Geri's morsel" in a work by the skald Einarr Skúlason). *Freki* is also used in a kenning for "carrion" ("Freki's meal") in a work by Þórðr Sjáreksson in chapter 58 of *Skáldskaparmál*.

Archaeological record

If the rider on horseback on the image on the Böksta Runestone has been correctly identified as Odin, then Geri and Freki are shown taking part in hunting an elk or moose.

Theories

A Vendel era bronze plate found on Öland, Sweden depicting a wolf-pelt warrior drawing a sword beside a dancing figure.

Freki is also a name applied to the monstrous wolf Fenrir in the *Poetic Edda* poem *Völuspá*. Folklorist John Lindow sees irony in the fact that Odin feeds one Freki at his dinner table and another—Fenrir—with his flesh during the events of Ragnarök.

Historian Michael Spiedel connects Geri and Freki with archaeological finds depicting figures wearing wolf-pelts and frequently found wolf-related names among the Germanic peoples, including Wulfhroc ("Wolf-Frock"), Wolfhetan ("Wolf-Hide"), Isangrim ("Grey-Mask"), Scrutolf ("Garb-Wolf") and Wolfgang ("Wolf-Gait"), Wolfdregil ("Wolf-Runner"), and Vulfolaic ("Wolf-Dancer") and myths regarding wolf warriors from Norse mythology (such as the Úlfhéðnar). Spiegel believes this to point to the pan-Germanic wolf-warrior band cult centered around Odin that waned away after Christianization.

Scholars have also noted Indo-European parallels to the wolves Geri and Freki as companions of a divinity. 19th century scholar Jacob Grimm observed a connection between this aspect of Odin's character and the Greek Apollo, to whom both the wolf and the raven are sacred. Philologist Maurice Bloomfield further connected the pair with the two dogs of Yama in Vedic Mythology, and saw them as a Germanic counterpart to a more general and widespread Indo-European "Cerberus"-theme. Michael Speidel finds similar parallels in the Vedic Rudra and the Roman Mars. Elaborating on the connection between wolves and figures of great power, he writes: "This is why Geri and Freki, the wolves at Woden's side, also glowered on the throne of the Anglo-Saxon kings. Wolf-warriors, like Geri and Freki, were not mere animals but mythical beings: as Woden's followers they bodied forth his might, and so did wolf-warriors."

References

Source (edited): "http://en.wikipedia.org/wiki/Geri_and_Freki"

Hati Hróðvitnisson

"Far away and long ago" (1920) by Willy Pogany.

In Norse mythology, **Hati Hróðvitnisson** (first name meaning "He Who Hates, Enemy") is a wolf that according to *Gylfaginning* chases the Moon across the night sky, just as the wolf Sköll chases the Sun during the day, until the time of Ragnarök when they will swallow these heavenly bodies, after which Fenrir will break free from his bonds and kill Odin.

Hati's surname is Hróðvitnisson, attested in both *Grímnismál* and *Gylfaginning*, which indicates that he is the son of Fenrir, whose alternate name is Hróðvitnir ("Famous Wolf"). Hati's mother is the giantess, not named but mentioned in *Völuspá* and *Gylfaginning*, who dwells to the east of Midgard in the forest of Járnviðr ("Ironwood"). Snorri Sturluson states that this giantess and witch bears many giants for sons, all in the form of wolves including one named Mánagarm ("Moon Hound") who shall swallow the Moon and is thus identified with Hati. From this passage it is also presumed that Sköll is Hati's brother.

Popular culture

- In January 2011, a wolf called Hati made an appearance in the online video game *RuneScape*.
- In one episode of Tiziano Sclavi's Dylan Dog, the Nightmare Investigator, Hati and his brother Sköll, were used as characters in tale N°289 "La via degli enigmi" ("The Way of Puzzles") and N°290 "L'erede Oscuro" ("The Dark Heir"); in which they are evil creatures who serve the main antagonist.
- Hati is one of the main characters as well as an important figure in mythology in the OFF-WHITE webcomic

Source (edited): "http://en.wikipedia.org/wiki/Hati_Hr%C3%B3%C3%B0vitnisson"

Mánagarmr

In Norse mythology, **Mánagarmr** ("Moon-Hound") is another name for the wolf Hati Hróðvitnisson, referring to his hunting down the moon during the Ragnarök and swallowing it. The name can be anglicized as *Managarm*, *Manegarm*, *Mánagarm* or *Managarmr*.

Snorri tells us that Managarm was born in a wood called Ironwood by an old witch giant, who gave birth to many wolf-like giant-children

Source (edited): "http://en.wikipedia.org/wiki/M%C3%A1nagarmr"

Sköll

"The Wolves Pursuing Sol and Mani" (1909) by J. C. Dollman.

"Far away and long ago" (1920) by Willy Pogany.

In Norse mythology, **Sköll** (Old Norse "Treachery") is a wolf that chases the horses Árvakr and Alsviðr, that drag the chariot which contains the sun (Sól) through the sky every day, trying to eat her. Sköll has a brother, Hati, who chases Máni, the moon. At Ragnarök, both Sköll and Hati will succeed in their quests.

Sköll, in certain circumstances, is used as a heiti to refer indirectly to the father (Fenrir) and not the son. This ambiguity works in the other direction also, for example in *Vafþrúðnismál*, where confusion exists in stanza 46 where Fenrir is given the sun-chasing attributes of his son Sköll. This can mostly be accounted for by the use of Hróðvitnir and Hróðvitnisson to refer to both Fenrir and his sons.

Popular culture

- Sköll is the name of a rare wolf character in World of Warcraft. The area he appears in is strongly influenced by Norse mythology.
- In one episode of Tiziano Sclavi's Dylan Dog, the Nightmare Investigator, Sköll and his brother Hati, were used as characters in tale N°289 "La via degli enigmi" ("The Way of Puzzles") and N°290 "L'erede Oscuro" ("The Dark Heir"); in which they are evil creatures who serve the main antagonist.
- In the 2nd season episode "Død Kalm" of The X-Files, Special Agent Dana Scully tells the story of Sköll in a voice-over.
- In the Anita Blake novels the Skoll and Hati are the enforcers of the Ulfric (Werewolf leader).
- In the MMORPG Runescape, Skolls brother Hati appeared during the winter to give double experience in any combat skill.
- Skoll is one of the main characters as well as an important figure in mythology in the OFF-WHITE webcomic
- A.A.S.R.Skøll is the name of the Amsterdam Student Rowing Club Skøll

==Notes==Skoll is the name of a popular beer in Brazil

Source (edited): "http://en.wikipedia.org/wiki/Sk%C3%B6ll"

Warg

A warg rider on an image stone from the former Hunnestad Monument

Hyrrokkin by Ludwig Pietsch (1865)

In Norse mythology, a **vargr** (often anglicised as **warg** or **varg**) is a wolf and in particular refers to the wolf Fenrir and his sons Sköll and Hati. Based on this, J. R. R. Tolkien in his fiction used the Old English form **warg** (other O.E. forms being **wearg** and **wearh**) to refer to a wolf-like creature of a particularly evil kind.

Etymology

In Old Norse, vargr is a term for "wolf" (*ulfr*). The Proto-Germanic **wargaz* meant "strangler" (see modern German *würgen*), and hence "evildoer, criminal, outcast." *Varg* is still the modern Swedish word for "wolf." Also cognate is Old English *warg* "large bear".

In line 1514 of Beowulf, Grendel's mother is described as a *grund-wyrgen* or "warg of the depths."

Norse mythology

In Norse mythology, wargs are in particular the mythological wolves Fenrir, Sköll and Hati. In the *Hervarar saga*, king Heidrek is asked by Gestumblindi (Odin),

What is that lamp
which lights up men,
but flame engulfs it,
and wargs grasp after it always.
Heidrek knows the answer is the Sun, explaining,
She lights up every land and shines over all men, and Skoll and Hatti are called wargs. Those are wolves, one going before the sun, the other after the moon. Wolves also served as mounts for more or less dangerous humanoid creatures. For instance, *Gunnr's horse* was a kenning for "wolf" on the Rök Runestone, in the *Lay of Hyndla*, the völva (witch) Hyndla rides a wolf, and to Baldr's funeral, the giantess Hyrrokin arrived on a wolf.

Tolkien's wargs

Taken from the Old English *warg*, the **wargs** or **wild wolves** are a race of fictional wolf creatures in J. R. R. Tolkien's books about Middle-earth. They are usually in league with the Orcs whom they permitted to ride on their backs into battle. It is probable that they are descended from Draugluin's werewolves, or of the wolf-hounds of the line of Carcharoth of the First Age. They are portrayed as somewhat intelligent, with a language of sorts, and are consciously in league with the Orcs, rather than wild animals the Orcs have tamed.

The concept of wolf-riding Orcs first appears in *The Tale of Tinúviel*, an early version of the story of Beren and Lúthien written in the 1920s, posthumously published as part of *The History of Middle-earth*.

In *The Hobbit*, the Wargs appear twice, once by working with Orcs (called goblins in the book), in hunting Bilbo Baggins, Gandalf, and the dwarves just east of the Misty Mountains, and once at the Battle of Five Armies.

In *The Lord of the Rings*, they are most prominently mentioned in the middle of *The Fellowship of the Ring*, where a band of Wargs, unaccompanied by Orcs, attacks the Fellowship in Eregion. During the War of the Ring in T.A. 3018–19, wolves prowled outside the walls of Bree. They are here distinguished from regular wolves "looking for food."

Adaptations

In the Rankin-Bass adaptation of *The Hobbit*, they are portrayed as larger than average wolves with ominously glowing eyes. Although Tolkien never gave a fully complete description of the Wargs (he simply noted that they were demonic wolves), they do seem to have a regular wolf-appearance in both *The Hobbit* and *The Lord of the Rings*, and they are regularly called "wolves."

In Peter Jackson's *Lord of the Rings* movie trilogy, a hyena-like, rather than wolf-like, design was chosen due to it looking more powerful.

They feature prominently in The Lord of the Rings Online, an MMO based on the works of Tolkien

In popular culture

Subsequent appearances of the creatures in popular culture often owe much to Tolkien. Similar to Tolkien's works, they are often depicted as evil, intelligent wolves that speak their own language, and are often allied with goblin tribes.

- In the *Dungeons & Dragons* roleplaying game, wargs appear as minor enemies.
- In the *A Song of Ice and Fire* fantasy novel series by George R. R. Martin, wargs are people who can form a telepathic-empathic bond with an animal. While this bond is active, the human perceives and experiences what the animal perceives/experiences.
- In David Clement-Davies's books The Sight and Fell, the wolves are known as the Varg, their self-chosen name. Furthermore, the Vargs' god is Fenris.
- Larry Correia's Monster Hunter International features giant wolf-like creatures used by orcs as mounts. However, the orcs of the MHI world are good and fight against the evil monsters. It is unclear whether these warg-like mounts are intelligent.
- In Jim Butcher's Codex Alera the leader of the Canim, a race of large anthropomorphic wolves, is named Varg.
- Wargs also appears often in the Castlevania video game series and are portrayed as big wolf like creatures appearing for the most part towards the beginning of the games. In the newest entry in the series Lords Of Shadow they are mounted by Lycan.
- In the MMORPG Ragnarok Online Renewal, Rangers can summon a warg as a mount.
- In Warcraft lore, the race Worgen are based on Wargs. Additionally, in World of Warcraft, the worg is a mob species closely related to the wolf; also, the orc racial mounts are large worgs.
- The song 'Unter der Eichen' (Under the oaks) of German folk metal band Equilibrium (band) describes a yearly ceremony. They sing, dance, drink and eat 'mehr noch als der größte Warg' (more than the greatest Warg).

Source (edited): "http://en.wikipedia.org/wiki/Warg"

Amarok (wolf)

Amarok is the name of a gigantic wolf in Inuit mythology.

It is said to hunt down and devour anyone foolish enough to hunt alone at night. Unlike real wolves who hunt in packs, Amarok hunts alone. It is sometimes considered equivalent to the waheela of cryptozoology.

Popular culture

- In the 1972 novel *Julie of the Wolves* by Jean Craighead George, the first alpha male of the Avalik River Pack is named 'Amaroq' by Miyax/Julie.

- A pack of 10 Amaroks appeared in the *The Secret Saturdays* episode "The Ice Caverns of Ellef Ringnes" with their vocal effects done by Fred Tatasciore.
Source (edited): "http://en.wikipedia.org/wiki/Amarok_(wolf)"

Asena

Asena (asenā) is the name of the one of the ten sons, whom mythical female wolf gave birth to, in old Turkic mythology. It is associated with a Göktürk ethnogenic myth "full of shamanic symbolism". But Ziya Gökalp mentioned to Asena in his article titled "Türk devletinin tekâmülü" (*Küçük Mecmua* magazine: that was published in 1922 in Diyarbakır) as follows: *According to Chinese people, Asena means wolf.* In Turkey many people believe that Asena should be the name of female wolf.

The Grey Wolf Legend

The legend runs as follows. After a battle, only an injured young boy survives. A she-wolf finds the injured child and nurses him back to health. He subsequently impregnates the wolf which then gives birth to ten half-wolf, half-human boys. One of these, Ashina, becomes their leader and founds the Ashina clan that ruled the Göktürks and other Turkic nomadic empires.

In 1930s when Turkish ethnic nationalism held its sway in Turkey, Bozkurt, Asena and Ergenekon were selected deliberately. Mustafa Kemal (Atatürk) used the motif of this legend. For example, on February 13, 1931, in the speech at Türkocağı in Malatya, he said *Turkish nation who will use railways [demiryolları], will have been honorable by showing the achievement of the first craftmanship and blacksmithy [demircilik] of its origin.*
Source (edited): "http://en.wikipedia.org/wiki/Asena"

Capitoline Wolf

The **Capitoline Wolf** (Latin: *Lupa Capitolina*) is a bronze sculpture of a she-wolf suckling twin infants, inspired by the legend of the founding of Rome. According to the legend, when Numitor, grandfather of the twins Romulus and Remus, was overthrown by his brother Amulius, the usurper ordered the twins to be cast into the Tiber River. They were rescued by a she-wolf who cared for them until a herdsman, Faustulus, found and raised them. The Capitoline Wolf has been housed since 1471 in the Museo Nuovo in the Palazzo dei Conservatori on the Campidoglio (the ancient Capitoline Hill), Rome, Italy.

The age and origin of the Capitoline Wolf is a subject of controversy. The statue was long thought to be an Etruscan work of the 5th century BC, with the twins added in the late 15th century AD, probably by the sculptor Antonio Pollaiolo. However, radiocarbon and thermoluminescence dating has found that it was possibly manufactured in the 13th century AD; this result, which undercuts the sculpture's iconic significance, is still contested, and while carbon dating has been performed on remnants of the casting core, the results have not yet been publicised (see below).

Description

The sculpture is somewhat larger than life-size, standing 75 cm high and 114 cm long. The wolf is depicted in a tense, watchful pose, with alert ears and glaring eyes watching for danger. By contrast, the human twins - executed in a completely different style - are oblivious to their surroundings, absorbed by their suckling.

Attribution and dating

The she-wolf from the legend of Romulus and Remus was regarded as a symbol of Rome from ancient times. Several ancient sources refer to statues depicting the wolf suckling the twins. Pliny the Elder mentions the presence in the Roman Forum of a statue of a she-wolf that was "a miracle proclaimed in bronze nearby, as though she had crossed the Comitium while Attus Navius was taking the omens". Cicero also mentions a statue of the she-wolf as one of a number of sacred objects on the Capitoline that had been inauspiciously struck by lightning in the year 65 BC: "it was a gilt statue on the Capitol of a baby being given suck from the udders of a wolf." Cicero also mentions the wolf in *De Divinatione* 1.20 and 2.47.

It was widely assumed that the Capitoline Wolf was the very sculpture described by Cicero, due to the presence of damage to the sculpture's paw, which was believed to correspond to the lightning strike of 65 BC. The 18th-century German art historian Johann Joachim Winckelmann attributed the statue to an Etruscan maker in the 5th century BC, based on how the wolf's fur was depicted. It was first attributed to the Veiian artist Vulca, who decorated the Temple of Jupiter Capitolinus, and then re-attributed to an unknown Etruscan artist of approximately 480-470 BC. Winckelmann correctly identified a Renaissance origin for the twins; they were probably added in 1471 or later.

During the 19th century a number of researchers questioned Winckelmann's dating of the bronze. August Emil Braun, the secretary of the Archaeological Institute of Rome, proposed in 1854 that the damage to the wolf's paw had been caused by an error during casting. Wilhelm Fröhner, the Conservator of the Louvre, stated in 1878 that style of the statue was attributable to the Carolingian period rather than the Etruscan, and in 1885 Wilhelm von Bode also stated that he was of the view that the statue was most likely a medieval work. However, these views were largely disregarded and had been forgotten by the 20th century.

In 2006 the Italian art historian Anna Maria Carruba and the Etruscologist Adriano La Regina contested the traditional dating of the wolf on the basis of an analysis of the casting technique. Carruba had been given the task of restoring the sculpture in 1997, enabling her to examine how it had been made. She observed that the statue had been cast in a single piece using a variation of the lost-wax casting technique that was not used in ancient times; ancient Greek and Roman bronzes were typically constructed from multiple pieces, a method that facilitated high quality castings with less risk than would be involved in casting the entire sculpture at once. Single-piece casting was, however, widely used in medieval times to mould bronze items that needed a high level of rigidity, such as bells and cannon. Carruba argues, like Braun, that the damage to the wolf's paw had resulted from an error in the moulding process. In addition, La Regina, who is the state superintendent of Rome's cultural heritage, argues that the sculpture's artistic style is more akin to Carolingian and Romanesque art than that of the ancient world.

Radiocarbon and thermoluminescence dating was carried out at the University of Salento in February 2007 to resolve the question. Although in July 2008 La Regina announced that the results of the tests had produced a "very precise indication in the 13th century",. The official results of the investigation were not to be disclosed before the end of 2008 but have, as of January 2011, not yet been published by the Museo Nuovo.

History of the sculpture

The sculpture in Musei Capitolini

It is unclear when the sculpture was first erected, but there are a number of medieval references to a "wolf" standing in the Pope's Lateran Palace. In the 10th century *Chronicon* of Benedict of Soracte, the monk chronicler writes of the institution of a supreme court of justice "in the Lateran palace, in the place called the Wolf, viz, the mother of the Romans." Trials and executions "at the Wolf" are recorded from time to time until 1438.

The twelfth-century English cleric Magister Gregorius wrote a descriptive essay *De Mirabilibus Urbis Romae* and recorded in an appendix three pieces of sculpture he had neglected: one was the Wolf in the portico at the principal entrance to the Vatican Palace. He mentions no twins, for he noted that she was set up as if stalking a bronze ram that was nearby, which served as a fountain. The wolf had also served as a fountain, Magister Gregorius thought, but it had been broken off at the feet and moved to where he saw it.

The present-day Capitoline Wolf could not have been the sculpture seen by Benedict and Gregorius, if its newly attributed age is accepted, though it is conceivable that it could have been a replacement for an earlier (now lost) depiction of the Roman wolf. In December 1471 Pope Sixtus IV ordered the present sculpture to be transferred to the Palazzo dei Conservatori on the Capitoline Hill, and the twins were added some time around then. The Capitoline Wolf joined a number of other genuinely ancient sculptures transferred at the same time, to form the nucleus of the Capitoline Museum.

Modern use and symbolism

The image was favored by Benito Mussolini, who cast himself as the founder of the "New Rome". To encourage American goodwill, he sent several copies of the Capitoline Wolf to U.S. cities. In 1929 he sent one replica for a Sons of Italy national convention in Cincinnati, Ohio. It was switched for another one in 1931, which still stands in Eden Park, Cincinnati. Another replica was given by Mussolini to the city of Rome, Georgia, the same year. A third copy went to Rome, New York.

The Capitoline Wolf was used on both the emblem and the poster for the 1960 Summer Olympics in Rome. The Roman football club A.S. Roma uses it in its emblem as well.

The programme of conservation undertaken in the 1990s resulted in an exhibition devoted to the *Lupa Capitolina* and her iconography.

In the 2009 movie *Agora*, set in fifth-century Alexandria, the Capitoline Wolf—complete with the del Pollaiolo twins—can be seen in the prefect's palace. This is visible in the scene before Hypatia's capture, directly behind her character.

Source (edited): "http://en.wikipedia.org/wiki/Capitoline_Wolf"

Chechen wolf

The wolf (Chechen: *Borz*, pronounced /boɾz/ or /bwoɾz/) is the national animal of the Chechen nation, and it is also the national embodiment. The national feeling of Chechens towards the wolf has many aspects.

As a poetic or symbolic comparison to the Chechen nation

The Chechen people are symbolically said to be variously related to wolves (not in a serious way, but in an either symbolic or joking manner), probably in relation to the "Wolf Mother" legend. Hence, characteristics of the wolf are also frequently compared to the Chechen people in a poetic sense, including the most famous line that members of the Chechen nation are "free and equal like wolves". Wolf clans are often equated to Chechen teips.

Chechen culture often emphasizes emulation of other characteristics of the wolf besides egalitarianism. As Jaimoukha explains in his ethnographic book on the Chechen people,

" According to the Chechen ethos, the wolf is the only animal that would enter into an unequal match, making up for any disadvantage by its agility, wit, courage and tenacity. If it loses the battle, it lies down facing the foe in full acceptance of its fate—Chechen poise equivalent to the famed British 'stiff upper lip'. "

There is a saying in the Chechen language describing a person, "He/She was raised by the She-Wolf" which implies the person has admirable personality traits.

Mythological

There is one myth that the mythological founder of the Chechen nation, Turpalo-Noxchuo (Chechen Hero, who Chechens are descended from "like sparks of steel"), was raised by a fabled, loving "Wolf Mother".

Old Chechen lore holds that the sheep was actually originally created for the wolf to enjoy, but man "stole" the sheep from the wolf (this is rather interesting considering that many Chechens in the past have in fact been shepherds). According to the ethnographic historian Jaimoukha, in olden times Chechens used to observe a wolf cult that would prevent lupine raids on sheep, by observing Saturday as being a special day.

In insignia and symbols

Chechen (Ichkerian) seal bearing a wolf, the nation's symbolic embodiment.

The wolf is frequently used for insignia and images, as a symbol of the Chechen nation. Common poses involve the wolf howling off the top of a mountain (Chechnya is very mountainous), laying down, or staring at the viewer.

The different poses evoke different symbolism:

- The wolf howling off the top of the mountain is usually an expression of national pride. In the period of 1991-1994, broadcasts in independent Chechnya bore this symbol, in that case symbolizing the struggle for national recognition. The symbol is also used by Chechens nowadays as a simple expression of being proud they are Chechen.
- The wolf laying down, facing the viewer is usually a reference to the mythological "Wolf Mother" of Turpalo-Noxchuo.
- Staring at the viewer usually evokes a feeling of intense emotion that the artist is implying they believe is felt by the Chechen nation.

Modernly, the coat of arms of the secular separatists in Chechnya bore the wolf. The Islamists later removed it and replaced it with Arabic script, and the Russian-sponsored ruling regime removed it entirely, but the secular government in exile still uses it. In addition, many other insignia of the Chechen nation (of all three governments) use the wolf as a heraldic symbol.

In naming

- The gun manufactured by the Chechen separatists in the two Chechen wars was called the Borz, after the wolf.

Source (edited): "http://en.wikipedia.org/wiki/Chechen_wolf"

MacQueen of Findhorn

MacQueen of Pall à Chrocain was a legendary Highland deer stalker popularly believed to have slain the last wolf in Scotland in 1743. The scene of the incident was Tarnaway Forest in the province of Morayshire in the county of Inverness. MacQueen received a message from his chief, the Laird of Clan Mackintosh, that a black wolf had killed two children whilst they were crossing the hills from Cawdor with their mother. MacQueen was requested to attend a "Tainchel" (a gathering to drive the country) at a tryst above Fi-Giuthas. In the morning, the Tainchel had long been assembled, though MacQueen was not initially present. When he arrived, MacQueen received a tirade of insulting comments for his delay, to which he asked "*Ciod e à chahbhag?*" (what was the hurry?). MacQueen lifted his plaid and produced the decapitated head of the wolf, tossing it in the middle of the surprised circle. MacQueen described to the assembly how he achieved the feat; "As I came through the *slochk* (ravine) by east the hill there, I foregathered wi' the beast. My long dog there turned him. I bucked wi' him, and dirkit him, and syne whuttled his craig (cut his throat), and brought awa' his countenance for fear he might come alive again, for they are very precarious creatures.

The chief rewarded him, giving him a land called Sean-achan "to yield good meat for his good greyhounds in all time coming". He later became chief of Clan MacQueen, and died in 1797.

Source (edited): "http://en.wikipedia.org/wiki/MacQueen_of_Findhorn"

Marchosias

In demonology, **Marchosias** is a powerful Great Marquis of Hell, commanding thirty legions of demons. He is a strong and excellent fighter and very reliable to the conjurer, giving true answers to all questions. Marchosias hoped after one thousand and two hundred years to return to heaven with the non-fallen angels, but he is deceived in that hope.

He is depicted as a wolf with a man's form as well as a griffon's wings and a serpent's tail, that under request changes shape into a man.

The name Marchosias comes from Late Latin *marchio*, marquis.

Other spellings: Marchocias.
Source (edited): "http://en.wikipedia.org/wiki/Marchosias"

The Boy Who Cried Wolf

The Boy Who Cried Wolf, is one of Aesop's Fables, numbered 210 in the Perry Index. From it is derived the English idiom 'to cry wolf', meaning to give a false alarm.

The fable and its history

Francis Barlow's illustration of the fable, 1687

The tale concerns a shepherd boy who tricks nearby villagers into thinking a wolf is attacking his flock. He repeats this so many times that when the sheep are actually confronted by a wolf, the villagers do not believe his cries for help and the flock is destroyed. The moral at the end of the Greek version is that 'the story shows that this is how liars are rewarded: even if they tell the truth, no one believes them.' This seems to echo a statement attributed to Aristotle by Diogenes Laërtius in his *The lives and opinions of eminent philosophers*, where the sage was asked what those who tell lies gain by it and he answered 'that when they speak truth they are not believed' William Caxton similarly closes his version with the remark that *men bileve not lyghtly hym whiche is knowen for a lyer.*

The story dates from Classical times but, since it was recorded only in Greek and not translated into Latin until the 15th century, it only began to gain currency after it appeared in Heinrich Steinhowel's collection of the fables and so spread through the rest of Europe. For this reason, there was no agreed title for the story. Caxton titles it "Of the child whiche kepte the sheep" (1484), Hieronymus Osius "The boy who lied" (*De mendace puero*, 1574), Francis Barlow "Of the herd boy and the farmers" (*De pastoris puero et agricolis*, 1687), Roger L'Estrange "A boy and false alarms" (1692), George Fyler Townsend "The shepherd boy and the wolf" (1867). It was under the final title that Edward Hughes set it as the first of ten "Songs from Aesop's fables" for children's voices and piano, in a poetic version by Peter Westmore (1965).

Teachers have used the fable as a cautionary tale about telling the truth but a recent educational experiment showed that reading "The Boy Who Cried Wolf" increased children's likelihood of lying, while a book on George Washington and the cherry tree decreased it dramatically. The suggestibility and favourable outcome of the behaviour described therefore seems the key to the moral nurture of the young. When dealing with the moral behaviour of adults, however, Samuel Croxall asks, with reference to political alarmism, 'when we are alarmed with imaginary dangers in respect of the public, till the cry grows quite stale and threadbare, how can it be expected we should know when to guard ourselves against real ones?'

The idiomatic phrase 'cry wolf' has been frequently used in the titles of films, books and lyrics, but these rarely refer directly to the fable.
Source (edited): "http://en.wikipedia.org/wiki/The_Boy_Who_Cried_Wolf"

Wolf of Gubbio

Saint Francis instructs the wolf, Carl Weidemeyer-Worpswede, 1911

The **wolf of Gubbio** was a wolf that , according to the *Fioretti di San Francesco,* terrorized the city of Gubbio until it was tamed by St. Francis of Assisi acting on behalf of God. The story is one of many in Christian narrative that depict holy persons exerting influence over animals and nature, a motif common to hagiography.

Story

During the period when Francis was living in Gubbio, a fierce wolf appeared in the country and began attacking livestock. Soon the wolf graduated to direct assaults on humans, and not long after began to dine upon them exclusively. It was known for lingering outside of the city gates in wait for anyone foolish enough to venture beyond them alone. No weapon was capable of inflicting injury upon the wolf, and all who attempted to destroy it were devoured. Eventually mere sight of the animal caused the entire city to raise alarm and the public refused to go outside the walls for any reason. It was at this point, when Gubbio was under siege, that Francis announced he was going to take leave and meet the wolf. He was advised against this more than once but, irrespective of the warnings, made the sign of the Cross and went beyond the gates with a small group of followers in tow. When he neared the lair of the wolf the crowd held back at a safe distance, but remained close enough to witness what transpired.

The wolf, having seen the group approach, rushed at Francis with its jaws open. Again Francis made the sign of the Cross and commanded the wolf to cease its attacks in the name of God, at which point the wolf trotted up to him docilely and lay at his feet, putting its head in his hands. The *Fioretti* then describes word-for-word his dealings with the wolf:

"Brother wolf, thou hast done much evil in this land, destroying and killing the creatures of God without his permission; yea, not animals only hast thou destroyed, but thou hast even dared to devour men, made after the image of God; for which thing thou art worthy of being hanged like a robber and a murderer. All men cry out against thee, the dogs pursue thee, and all the inhabitants of this city are thy enemies; but I will make peace between them and thee, O brother wolf, is so be thou no more offend them, and they shall forgive thee all thy past offences, and neither men nor dogs shall pursue thee any more."

The wolf bowed its head and submitted to Francis, completely at his mercy.

"As thou art willing to make this peace, I promise thee that thou shalt be fed every day by the inhabitants of this land so long as thou shalt live among them; thou shalt no longer suffer hunger, as it is hunger which has made thee do so much evil; but if I obtain all this for thee, thou must promise, on thy side, never again to attack any animal or any human being; dost thou make this promise?"

In agreement, the wolf placed one of its forepaws in Francis' outstretched hand, and the oath was made. Francis then commanded the wolf to return with him to Gubbio. Meanwhile the townsfolk, having heard of the miracle, gathered in the city marketplace to await Francis and his companion, and were shocked to see the ferocious wolf behaving as though his pet. When Francis reached the marketplace he offered the assembled crowd an impromptu sermon with the tame wolf at his feet. He is quoted as saying: "How much we ought to dread the jaws of hell, if the jaws of so small an animal as a wolf can make a whole city tremble through fear?" With the sermon ended Francis renewed his pact with the wolf publicly, assuring it that the people of Gubbio would feed it from their very doors if it ceased its depredations. Once more the wolf placed its paw in Francis' hand.

Francis leading the wolf to Gubbio

Aftermath

Thereafter Gubbio venerated Francis and he received great praise from its citizens. Many of them were convinced by the miracle and offered their thanks to God, going on to be converted. This episode in the *Fioretti* is concluded with a note that the wolf lived for a further two years at Gubbio, going from home to home for sustenance and honoring the provisions of its agreement with Francis. At its death the city was saddened, for even though it had slain so many it was a symbol of the sanctity of Francis and the power of God. The National Gallery, London has a polyptych by Sassetta in the Sainsbury Wing, depicting scenes from the life of Saint Francis, and it includes a scene depicting Saint Francis making a pact with the Wolf.

Source (edited): "http://en.wikipedia.org/wiki/Wolf_of_Gubbio"

Wolves in folklore, religion and mythology

Wolves appear in folklore and mythological traditions around the world. Symbolism of the wolf varies: a hungry Shadow self, a Trickster, or a demonic presence. Some cultures believe humans descend from wolves (see below), and the wolf may have a protective quality as well.

Mythology

Hindu mythology

Wolves are occasionally mentioned in Hindu mythology. In the *Harivamsa*, Krishna, to convince the people of Vraja to migrate to Vrindavan, creates hundreds of wolves from his hairs, which frighten the inhabitants of Vraja into making the journey. In the *Rig Veda*, Rijrsava is blinded by his father as punishment for having given 101 of his family's sheep to a she-wolf, who in turn prays to the Ashvins to restore his sight. Bhima, the voracious son of the god Vayu, is described as *Vrikodara*, meaning "wolf-stomached".

Turkic and Mongolian mythology

In Altaic mythology of the Turkic and Mongolian peoples, the wolf is a revered animal. The shamanic Turkic peoples even believed they were descendants of wolves in Turkic legends. The legend of Asena is an old Turkic myth that tells of how the Turkic people were created. In Northern China a small Turkic village was raided by Chinese soldiers, but one small baby was left behind. An old she-wolf with a sky-blue mane named Asena found the baby and nursed him, then the she-wolf gave birth to half wolf, half human cubs therefore the Turkic people were born. Also in Turkic mythology it is believed that a gray wolf showed the Turks the way out of their legendary homeland *Ergenekon*, which allowed them to spread and conquer their neighbours. In modern Turkey this myth inspired extreme-right nationalist groups known as "Grey Wolves". In Mongolian folk medicine, eating the intestines of a wolf is said to alleviate chronic indigestion, while sprinkling food with powdered wolf rectum is said to cure hemorroids. Some Mongolians believe that Chinggis Khan was the product of a union by a blue wolf and a deer. Mongol mythology explains the wolf's occasional habit of surplus killing by pointing to their traditional creation story. It states that when God explained to the wolf what it should and should not eat, he told it that it may eat one sheep out of 1,000. The wolf however misunderstood and thought God said kill 1,000 sheep and eat one.

Roman mythology

The Capitoline Wolf with Romulus and Remus. Musei Capitolini, Palazzo dei Conservatori, Rome.

According to the Roman tradition, a wolf was responsible for the childhood survival of the future founders of Rome, Romulus and Remus. The twin babies were ordered to be killed by their great uncle Amulius. The servant ordered to kill them, however, relented and placed the two on the banks of the Tiber river. The river, which was in flood, rose and gently carried the cradle and the twins downstream, where under the protection of the river deity Tiberinus, they would be adopted by a she-wolf known as *Lupa* in Latin, an animal sacred to Mars.

The comedian Plautus used the image of wolves to ponder the cruelty of man as a wolf unto man.

Finnish mythology

Unlike fox and bear, the wolf has always been feared and hated in Finland, and wolf has been the symbol of destruction and desolation, to the extent that the very name of wolf in Finnish language, *susi*, means also "a useless thingie" and the by-name *hukka* means perdition and annihilation. While bear has been the sacred animal of Finns, wolves have always been hunted and killed mercilessly. The wolf has been represented as implacable and malicious predator, killing more than it manages to eat.

Norse mythology

Fenrir, bound by the gods.

Norse mythology prominently includes three malevolent wolves, in particular: the giant Fenrisulfr or Fenrir, eldest child of Loki and Angrboda who was feared and hated by the Æsir, and Fenrisulfr's children, Sköll and Hati. Fenrir is bound by the gods, but is ultimately destined to grow too large for his bonds and devour Odin during the course of Ragnarök. At that time, he will have grown so large that his upper jaw touches the sky while his lower touches the earth when he gapes. He will be slain by Odin's son, Viðarr, who will either stab him in the heart or rip his jaws asunder according to different accounts. Fenrir's two offspring will according to legend, devour the sun and moon at Ragnarök. On the other hand, however, the wolves Geri and Freki were the Norse god Odin's faithful pets who were reputed to be "of good omen."

In the Hervarar saga, king Heidrek is asked by Gestumblindi (Odin),

*What is that lamp
which lights up men,
but flame engulfs it,
and wargs grasp after it always.*

Heidrek knows the answer is the Sun, explaining

She lights up every land and shines over all men, and Skoll and Hatti are called wargs. Those are wolves, one going before the sun, the other after the moon.

But wolves also served as mounts for more or less dangerous humanoid creatures. For instance, *Gunnr's horse* was a kenning for "wolf" on the Rök Runestone, in the Lay of Hyndla, the völva (witch) Hyndla rides a wolf, and to Baldr's funeral, the giantess Hyrrokin arrived on a wolf.

Baltic mythology

According to legend, the establishment of the Lithuanian capital Vilnius began when the grand duke Gediminas dreamt of an iron wolf howling near the hill.

Chechen mythology

In Chechen (and generally also Ingush) lore, wolves are almost always portrayed in a positive light, either as an equivalent for the nation, or as the loving "Wolf Mother". The Chechen people are symbolically said to be variously related to wolves (not in a serious way, but in an either symbolic or joking manner), probably in relation to the "Wolf Mother" legend. Hence, characteristics of the wolf are also frequently compared to the Chechen people in a poetic sense, including the most famous line that members of the Chechen nation are "free and equal like wolves". Given this reverence for the wolf, it is easily the most common symbol used by Chechen nationalists.

Wolf clans are often equated to Chechen teips. The wolf for Chechens is not only the national animal, but also the national embodiment, and the wolf is frequently used to show pride. It is notable that the equation of "wolves = Chechens" also in some ways relates to the Chechen character, as it reflects the way Chechens see themselves (and to a degree, how others see them): intelligent, organized in clans, loyal, and brave.

The point of Chechens being "related" to wolves even goes to the point of the national founding myth- Turpalo-Noxchuo, the "founder" of the Chechen nation in legend, was raised by the Wolf Mother. It is also said that Chechens are descended from Turpalo-Noxchuo and the Wolf Mother like "sparks off steel".

Japanese mythology

In Japan, grain farmers once worshiped wolves at shrines and left food offerings near their dens, beseeching them to protect their crops from wild boars and deer. Talismans and charms adorned with images of wolves were thought to protect against fire, disease, and other calamities and brought fertility to agrarian communities and to couples hoping to have children. The Ainu people believed that they were born from the union of a wolflike creature and a goddess.

Native American mythology

Helmet and collar representing a wolf, at the Museum of the Americas in Madrid. Made of wood, shell and made in the 18th century by tlingit indigenous people, from the North American Pacific Northwest Coast. Tlingit people admired and feared wolves because of their strength and violence.

Wolves were generally revered by tribes that survived by hunting, but were thought little of by those that survived through agriculture. Some tribes, such as the Nunamiut of northern and northwestern Alaska and the Naskapi of Labrador respected the wolf's hunting skill and tried to emulate the wolf in order to hunt successfully. Others see the wolf as a guide. The Tanaina of Alaska believed that wolves were once men, and viewed them as brothers.

In the Cardinal directions of the Plains Indians, the wolf represented the west, while for the Pawnee, it represented the southeast. According to the Pawnee creation myth, the wolf was the first creature to experience death. The Wolf Star, enraged at not having been invited to attend a council on how the Earth should be made, sent a wolf to steal the whirlwind bag of The Storm that Comes out of the West, which contained the first humans. Upon being freed from the bag, the humans killed the wolf, thus bringing death into the world. The Pawnee, being both an agricultural and hunting people, associated the wolf with both corn and the bison; the "birth" and "death" of the Wolf Star (Sirius) was to them a reflection of the wolf's coming and going down the path of the Milky Way known as Wolf Road.

Wolves were not always portrayed positively in Native American cultures. The Netsilik Inuit and Takanaluk-arnaluk believed that the sea-woman Nuliayuk's home was guarded by wolves. The Naskapi's believed that the caribou afterlife is guarded by giant wolves that kill careless hunters who venture too near. The Navajo people feared witches in wolf's clothing called "Mai-cob". Wolves were feared by the Tsilhqot'in, who believed that contact with wolves

Religion

Christianity

A mosaic on the entrance of a Church in Denmark depicting the Good Shepherd protecting a lamb from a wolf

The Bible contains 13 references to wolves, usually as metaphors for greed and destructiveness. In the New Testament, Jesus is quoted to have used wolves as illustrations to the dangers His followers would have faced should they follow him (Matthew 10:16, Acts 10:29, Matthew 7:15)

Virgil leads Dante away from the She-Wolf in *Inferno* Canto 1 lines 87-88 as drawn by Gustave Doré for the elephant folio edition in early 1861

The Book of Genesis was interpreted in Medieval Europe as stating that nature exists solely to support man (Genesis 1:29), who must cultivate it (Genesis 2:15), and that animals are made for his own purposes (Genesis 2:18-20). By this perspective, nature was only acceptable if controlled by man. The wolf is repeatedly mentioned in the scriptures as an enemy of flocks: a metaphor for evil men with a lust for power and dishonest gain, as well as a metaphor for Satan preying on innocent God-fearing Christians, contrasted with the shepherd Jesus who keeps his flock safe. The Roman Catholic Church often used the negative imagery of wolves to create a sense of real devils prowling the real world. Quoting from Leviticus and Deuteronomy, the *Malleus Maleficarum* states that wolves are either agents of God sent to punish sinners, or agents of the Devil sent with God's blessing to harass true believers to test their faith.

However, legends surrounding Saint Francis of Assisi show him befriending a wolf. According to the *Fioretti*, the city of Gubbio was besieged by the Wolf of Gubbio, which devoured both livestock and men. Francis of Assisi, who was living in Gubbio at the time took pity on the townsfolk, and went up into the hills to find the wolf. Soon fear of the animal had caused all his companions to flee, but the saint pressed on and when he found the wolf he made the sign of the cross and commanded the wolf to come to him and hurt no one. Miraculously the wolf closed his jaws and lay down at the feet of St. Francis. *"Brother Wolf, you do much harm in these parts and you have done great evil..."* said Francis. *"All these people accuse you and curse you... But brother wolf, I would like to make peace between you and the people."* Then Francis led the wolf into the town, and surrounded by startled citizens he made a pact between them and the wolf. Because the wolf had *"done evil out of hunger"* the townsfolk were to feed the wolf regularly, and in return, the wolf would no longer prey upon them or their flocks. In this manner Gubbio was freed from the menace of the predator. Francis, ever the lover of animals, even made a pact on behalf of the town dogs, that they would not bother the wolf again.

In Canto I of Dante's *Inferno*, the Pilgrim encounters a She-Wolf blocking the path to a hill bathed in light. The She-Wolf represents the sins of concupiscence and incontinence. She is prophecised by the shade of Virgil to one day be sent to Hell by a greyhound.

Islam

Wolves are mentioned three times in the Qur'an, specifically in the Sura Yusuf.

12.13: *"He said: Surely it grieves me that you should take him off, and I fear lest the wolf devour him while you are heedless of him."*

12.14: *"They said: Surely if the wolf should devour him notwithstanding that we are a (strong) company, we should then certainly be losers."*

12.17: *"They said: O our father! Surely we went off racing and left Yusuf by our goods, so the wolf devoured him, and you will not believe us though we are truthful."*

Mormonism

John 10. 12: *"But he that is an hireling, and not the shepherd, whose own the sheep are not, seeth the wolf coming, and leaveth the sheep, and fleeth: and the wolf catcheth them, and scattereth the sheep."*

Alma 5. 59-60: *"For what shepherd is there among you having many sheep doth not watch over them, that the wolves enter not and devour his flock? And behold, if a wolf enter his aflock doth he not drive him out? Yea, and at the last, if he can, he will destroy him. And now I say unto you that the good shepherd doth call after you; and if you will hearken unto his voice he will bring you into his fold, and ye are his sheep; and he commandeth you that ye suffer no ravenous wolf to enter among you, that ye may not be destroyed."*

Gen. 49. 27: *"Benjamin shall ravin as a wolf: in the morning he shall devour the prey, and at night he shall divide the spoil."*

Isa. 11. 6: *"The wolf also shall dwell with the lamb, and the leopard shall lie down with the kid; and the calf and the young lion and the fatling together; and a little child shall lead them."* This is repeated in chapter 21 of the Second book of Nephi.

Isa. 65. 25: *"The wolf and the lamb shall feed together, and the lion shall eat straw like the bullock: and dust shall be the serpent's meat. They shall not hurt nor destroy in all my holy mountain, saith the Lord."*

Jer. 5. 6: *"Wherefore a lion out of the forest shall slay them, and a wolf of the bevenings shall spoil them, a leopard shall watch over their cities: every one that goeth out thence shall be torn in pieces: because their transgressions are many, and their backslidings are increased."*

Ne. 30. 12: *"And then shall the wolf dwell with the lamb; and the leopard shall lie down with the kid, and the calf, and the young lion, and the fatling, together; and a little child shall lead them."*

Other symbolism

With the ever expanding growth of Scandinavian based heavy metal, the wolf has been commonly used throughout visual and audio imagery. Bands such as Sonata Arctica (who use the wolf as their "mascot"), Marduk, Wintersun, and Wolf, whose logo contains the image of a wolf paw, have used the wolf throughout their lyrics. The symbol of the wolf has been reputed to represent varying degrees of power as well as connections to Nordic countries (such as Denmark, Finland, Norway, and Sweden) and their natural habitats (snow, mountains, and forests). Additionally, images of wolves can be more violent, with the focus on their potential ferocity and ability to hunt.

Source (edited): "http://en.wikipedia.org/wiki/Wolves_in_folklore,_religion_and_mythology"

Wolves in heraldry

Coat of arms of Łobez

The **wolf** was widely used in many forms in heraldry during the medieval period. Though commonly reviled as a livestock predator and man-eater, the wolf was also considered a noble and courageous animal, and frequently appeared on the Arms and crests of numerous noble families. It typically symbolised the rewards of perseverance in long sieges or hard industry.

History

British Isles and other Anglophone heraldries

Wolves appeared frequently in English heraldry. A shield bearing two wolf heads was attributed to the Earl of Chester, circa 1070. "Two wolf's heads erased azure" were later used on the arms of subsequent Earls.

Edward IV (1442–83) used a white wolf for one of his badges, along with a white lion, denoting his descent from the House of Mortimer.

The wolf or his head is often used for canting on names such as Videlou, de Lou (both recorded in the anonymous *Great Roll* of 1308–14), Lupus (in the reign of Edward III), Wolferston (in the *Henry VI Roll*, circa 1422–61), Wolseley, Lovett, Low, Lovell, Lupton and of course Wolfe.

Wolves are to be found
- **rampant** in the coat of Louth Town Council (England)
- **demi** in the crest of Peter John Crabtree (Canada)
- **demi** and **winged** in the crest of Walter William Roy Bradford (Canada)
- **heads** only in the coat of James Thomas Flood (Canada)
- as **supporters** in the bearings of the Corporation of the Municipality of Greenstone, Ontario
- in the **Salish style** in the coat of the Village of Belcarra, British Columbia

The "Enfield beast", an imaginary creature with the combined characteristics of wolves, foxes and eagles, appears as the crest of the Irish family of Kelly and is also used in the coat and as a supporter for the former Enfield Borough Council and its successor the London Borough of Enfield (England).

Continental Europe

A Spanish depiction of a heraldic wolf

The wolf is also featured in the heraldry of continental European nations. Spanish heraldry often represented wolves carrying the bodies of lambs in their mouths or across their backs.

Wolves are also common in German heraldry. The town of Passau (Bavaria) bears a red wolf rampant on a white shield. In Saxony, a black wolf rampant on a yellow shield features on the crest of von Wolfersdorf family. A green wolf grasping a dead swan in its jaws on a yellow shield is depicted on the crest and Arms of the Counts von Brandenstein-Zeppelin.

Wolves in heraldry

Chechen (Ichkerian) seal bearing a wolf, the nation's symbolic embodiment.

In Italian heraldry, the attributed arms of Romulus and Remus were said to depict the Capitoline Wolf. An undated Milanese badge allegedly in the Biblioteca Trivulziana, Milan, shows a lamb lying on its back with a wolf standing over it.

In French heraldry, the Wolfcatcher Royal had as his official insignia two wolf heads facing frontally.

A horned, wolf-like creature called the Calopus or Chatloup was at one time connected with the Foljambe and Cathome family.

Modernly, the coat of arms of the secular separatists in Chechnya bore the wolf, because the wolf (borz) is the Chechen (or Ichkerian) nation's national embodiment. The Islamists later removed it, and the Russian-sponsored ruling regime removed it entirely, but the secular government in exile still uses. In addition, many other insignia of the Chechen nation (of all three governments) use the wolf as a heraldic symbol. Not only is it the national animal, but the Chechen people are symbolically said to be variously related to wolves (not in a serious way, but in an either symbolic or joking manner), and there are legends of their ancestors being raised by a "wolf mother". Characteristics of the wolf are also frequently compared to the Chechen people in a poetic sense, including the most famous line that members of the Chechen nation are "free and equal like wolves".

Source (edited): "http://en.wikipedia.org/wiki/Wolves_in_heraldry"